Artful Cards

Artful Cards

60 Fresh & Fabulous Designs

Katherine Duncan Aimone

LARK BOOKS

A Division of Sterling Publishing Co., Inc.
New York

Art Director: Susan McBride

Layout & Production: Thom Gaines

Photography: Keith Wright

Illustrations: Orrin Lundgren

Cover Designer: Barbara Zaretsky

Assistant Editor: Rebecca Guthrie

Associate Art Director: Shannon Yokeley

Editorial Assistance: Delores Gosnell

Editorial Interns: Metta L. Pry, Kelly J. Johnson

The Library of Congress has cataloged the hardcover edition as follows:

Duncan-Aimone, Katherine
    Artful cards : 60 fresh & fabulous designs / Katherine Duncan Aimone.
        p. cm.
    Includes index.
    ISBN 1-57990-551-X (hardcover)
    1. Greeting cards. I. Title. II. Title: Artful cards, 60 fresh and fabulous designs. III. Title: Artful cards, sixty fresh & fabulous designs.
TT872.D96 2005
745.594'1—dc22   2005012493

10 9 8 7 6 5 4 3 2 1

Published by Lark Books, A Division of
Sterling Publishing Co., Inc.
387 Park Avenue South, New York, N.Y. 10016

First Paperback Edition 2007
© 2005, Lark Books

Distributed in Canada by Sterling Publishing,
c/o Canadian Manda Group, 165 Dufferin Street
Toronto, Ontario, Canada M6K 3H6

Distributed in the United Kingdom by GMC Distribution Services,
Castle Place, 166 High Street, Lewes, East Sussex, England BN7 1XU

Distributed in Australia by Capricorn Link (Australia) Pty Ltd.,
P.O. Box 704, Windsor, NSW 2756 Australia

If you have questions or comments about this book, please contact:
Lark Books, 67 Broadway, Asheville, NC 28801.
Tel. (828) 253-0467

Manufactured in China

ISBN 13: 978-1-57990-551-4 (hardcover) 978-1-60059-140-2 (paperback)
ISBN 10: 1-57990-551-X (hardcover) 1-60059-140-X (paperback)

For information about custom editions, special sales, premium and
corporate purchases, please contact Sterling Special Sales Department
at 800-805-5489 or specialsales@sterlingpub.com.

contents

card projects

Introduction

Let's face it…we all *love* to receive cards. And some of us love to *make* cards. I'll never forget the first time I made a card in kindergarten. Totally enamored with red construction paper, my heart leapt at the prospect of making it into *something*… something magical created by me. I grabbed small scissors and tenderly cut the paper into a raggedy-edged heart.

Glue squashed out around the contours of the heart when I pressed it on the front of my awkwardly folded card. I wiped away some of it with my sleeve and then stopped suddenly, realizing the unexpected opportunity to douse the sticky edges with yummy gold glitter.

I sprinkled a healthy portion of glitter on it, and then gasped softly when I saw the heart outlined with a sparkling gold line. With new confidence, I squeezed blobs of glue all over the center of the heart and trickled tiny sequins into the receptive white pools. Now my creation was lovelier than ever!

Later, I experienced the joy of giving it to someone I loved….

When you think about it, it's the thoughtfulness that goes into making something for a loved one that matters. Humble materials are all you need. If I'm ever at a loss on where to start on a new art project, I can always get ideas by making a card or gift for someone else. Giving truly is the most enjoyable part of creating.

—Lynn Whipple

When I make cards today for friends or family, I can still tap into this emotional and creative reservoir from years ago. Cards are a simple and wonderful way of giving to others. In a manufactured world, we're starved for the personal touch. We secretly long to receive things that have time, not just money, invested in them. Handmade cards are often saved for years because of the care put into them by the giver.

Most cards don't take much time or space to create and aren't expensive. In fact, it's usually more economical to make your own cards than to buy them off a rack. Cards are like small blank canvases waiting to be embellished. But you don't need the skills of an artist to create them.

This book is filled to the brim with interesting card projects.

The technical aspects range from very simple to more complex. The wide range of interpretations by accomplished artists and designers includes collage, scrapbooking, stitching on paper, stamping, and beading. You'll also learn how to make some dimensional or pop-up cards.

If you want to make a certain card, you'll have detailed instructions at your disposal, along with a list of materials and tools. If you're already an avid card-maker who doesn't need much instruction, you'll find a wealth of fresh ideas to inspire you.

Begin now. Flip through the pages that follow and let your mind roam. Pick out a design that appeals to you. Gather your supplies and make a card to give away that will repay you in ways you never imagined.

Cardmaking Basics

If you look through the following chapter, you'll find that it serves as a handy reference as you work on card projects. You needn't read through all of it before you begin.

All of the papers, tools, materials, and supplies discussed relate to the projects in this book. Use this chapter as your guide, but don't get overwhelmed. If you're just beginning, start with a few simple things, and add to your stock as you discover where your interests lie.

In this chapter you'll also learn about techniques, such as how to make your own cards and envelopes, as well as some of the most popular decorating techniques used by contemporary cardmakers. In essence, you only need one caveat about cardmaking and its many possibilities: once you've begun, you won't want to stop!

Cards, Paper, and Envelopes

Even though selecting papers for cards can seem slightly overwhelming because of all the choices you'll have, simply think of this process as a grand adventure. Paper is the basis for most cards and is used as the substrate (the "canvas" that supports your design) as well as an embellishment material.

The Basic Card

When you're choosing or making a basic paper card, think about the weight of the paper. Some of this is just common sense. For instance, if you're going to glue a lot of layers on the front of the card or add embellishments, you'll need a heavier weight card stock or paper.

To help you decide, just pick up a piece of the paper in the store and feel it. Does it seem substantial enough to hold layers of other papers or embellishments without sagging under pressure? Or, if you're going to fold it into something more detailed than a simple card, will it be too thick to fold? If you're not sure, fold a sheet to test it out before buying a lot of it.

When you fold over a machine-made paper, you'll discover the grain or the direction of the fibers. When you fold the paper into a card, it's important to go with the grain rather than against it to create a clean fold. This is especially important if you're making a card with multiple folds.

For most cards, you'll be safe with a good quality cover-weight paper or card stock. Card stock is available in loads of colors at craft or art supply, scrapbooking, stamping, or stationery stores. If you're just beginning to experiment with cardmaking, try buying basic white or off-white cards so that you can use them for all types of designs without the added consideration of the card's color.

Card stock is usually sold flat or already folded into cards that are neatly cut or have deckled (torn) edges with accompanying envelopes. Needless to say, you might prefer prefolded cards so that you can get on with the creative part of the experience. They're available in many colors and styles. But if you want to create a specific size or shape that is not produced commercially, you can easily cut card stock and score it with a bone folder (see page 18).

Handmade papers make a great choice for distinctive cards because of their unique textures and varied surfaces. They can be pricey, but are well worth the cost for special projects. Keep in mind that they are not as predictable and consistent as commercial papers and have no grain. Their artistic look is what makes them desirable.

If you're planning to use inks or watercolors for lettering or drawing, it's important to use paper made for those purposes for your basic card. Acid-free, well-sized paper with a high-rag content is the best paper to use. These papers are made with cotton fibers rather than wood pulp. On the other hand, if you're just doodling with colored pens, you can use just about any kind of paper that takes the ink.

If you're investing a lot of time in a lettered or inked piece, begin by using layout bond paper to practice your lettering or other design before inking or painting in the final letters on good paper. You can duplicate this perfected original if you're sending out multiples of it.

Decorative, Collage, and Scrapbooking Papers

This is a subject that won't put you to sleep! The current craze over making scrapbooks, altering books, and doing collage has resulted in more papers to choose from than ever. In the old days, you'd have to find an art supply or stationery store to get anything more exotic than typing paper, but now papers are available in many places—not only craft and art supply stores but the Internet and beyond. Printed with a plethora of designs, they can be textured, embossed, you name it...there's a paper out there to fit every yearning you have. You can even buy papers that resemble fabric or leather.

Nevertheless, keep in mind that all papers aren't created equal. Keep the purpose of the card in mind, and you'll be able to make wise choices to fit your budget. For instance, if you're making a single card that you hope the recipient will save, you'll probably want to buy more expensive archival papers, perhaps even handmade papers. But if you're making a bucketful of cards for a party, what does it matter if you use inexpensive papers? You can cut, paste, and experiment with no concerns about your pocketbook.

The more you learn about papers, the more of a connoisseur you'll become. You'll learn to differentiate between them and appreciate the finer ones. You might find yourself collecting special papers and saving them. Just spreading out a collection of beautiful and varied papers on a table can serve as a springboard for great ideas.

Vellum

Traditional vellum is made from animal skin and is extremely pricey. Paper vellum, however, is reasonably priced. It is a tough, translucent material that comes in a variety of colors, patterns, and finishes. This popular paper is often used to veil images and create an intriguing layered effect.

You can print out invitations or other multiples on laser-compatible vellum to serve as elegant enclosures or overlays for the front of a patterned card. Vellum envelopes are also available in lots of sizes and colors.

Found Papers, Photos, and Ephemera

For our purposes, this category includes all recycled papers such as old magazines, photos, pages from old books, envelopes with great-looking postage stamps, postcards, junk mail, manufactured greeting cards, old dress patterns—you get the picture! These materials are the staples of traditional collage artists.

The archival quality of many of the commercial papers in this category isn't very good, since the papers are inexpensive and made for the moment. But for most cards that you send out, these papers will last as long as needed.

Envelopes

When you buy blank folded cards, they'll usually come with nice envelopes that match. These come in every imaginable size, color, and shape. Some even have interesting fasteners instead of a traditional flap. You can also find alternative envelopes made from fabric, hemp, and other materials. These are especially nice if you've made a dimensional piece that you plan to hand directly to the recipient without mailing it.

In addition to this, you can buy small boxes or envelopes that have added depth for holding highly embellished cards. And, if you want to be really inventive, try recycling something such as a flat candy tin or a plastic CD cover to hold your card.

If you make your own cards, you can also make your own envelopes. An easy way to do this is to unseal a commercial envelope of the style and size you want, and trace the flat piece on the paper you plan to use. Cut out the envelope, and then mark the position of the folds. Use a bone folder to score and fold them. If you can't find a commercial envelope in the exact size you want, you can simply size another one up or down, while still using the basic design as your guide.

You can also use envelope templates that can be bought through craft supply stores or various Internet sites. In this book, we provide you with several templates that match specific cards.

Tools

The tools described here range from a simple pair of scissors to a heat gun! Again, you don't need many tools to make cards, but there are some that can make your endeavors a whole lot easier. Begin with scissors, a craft knife and cutting mat, and a ruler.

Craft Knife

You'll find yourself reaching for your craft knife quite often when making cards. This tool works well for making very accurate small cuts such as windows and small shapes. Always keep a set of fresh blades on hand, since a dull blade will drag and leave a ragged edge. Choose a version that's easy to grip, and hold the knife at a 45° angle to create crisp cuts.

Ruler, Square, and Triangle

To guide the craft knife, use a metal ruler or other ruling device. A steel square is also great to have on hand, especially if you're squaring and cutting larger sheets of paper. Triangles come in handy for scoring and cutting paper shapes.

Cutting Mat or Glass

Always place a self-healing cutting mat beneath the paper you're cutting with a craft knife. It will protect the blades of the knife while keeping the papers from curling. Because it's marked with a measuring grid, it can also be used like a ruler. As an alternative, you can cut paper on a sheet of glass, which some cardmakers prefer. Tape the edges of the glass to protect your fingers.

Scissors

You'll find that you frequently use scissors to cut sheets of paper and small decorative items. Keep both a long-bladed and short-bladed pair on hand for different needs. Make

sure that the ones you choose are lightweight and comfortable to hold. The blades should always be sharp and clean, just like the blades of your craft knife. If glue gets on the blades, remove it before cutting again.

Bone Folder

This bookbinding tool is essential for scoring paper and smoothing out creases if you're making folded cards. Bone folders are made from actual bone, resin, or wood. They come in several sizes.

Decorative-edged Scissors

You'll find many uses for these scissors that cut a variety of different edges. You can use them simply because you like the look they create, or to emulate the edges of things such as old photos, postage stamps, or even fabric rickrack.

Paper Cutter

Remember that paper cutter with the large swinging arm (the guillotine!) that your teacher taught you

to steer clear of in grade school? If you have access to one of these, it's perfect for dividing up larger sheets of paper to make cards. And buying larger sheets can save you money if you're making a lot of cards.

Paper Trimmer

This handy piece of equipment is smaller than the traditional paper cutter. It's great for cutting cards or papers to size.

Tapes

You can use clear double-sided tape to adhere decorative pieces to cards. Foam tape is great for creating a three-dimensional effect, since it lifts the element off the card. And you can use dimensional double-stick dots to hold smaller pieces in place. Use low-tack artist's tape to temporarily hold pieces on the surface while you work out a design, since this tape leaves no residue behind.

Glue Brushes

Use inexpensive brushes for applying water-based liquid adhesives. Slightly stiff, flat, synthetic brushes work well for this purpose. Keep different sizes on hand for various applications. Designate them for glue only, and make sure to rinse them out with warm water after using them.

Awl

An awl is a small pointed tool that can be used to punch small holes in paper for hand stitching. It can also be used to mark lines that you plan to cut.

Hole and Shaped Punches

The traditional round hole punch from an office supply store comes in handy for punching small holes in sheets of paper, and a circle cutter can be adjusted to cut circles in a range of diameters. Square punches are great for cutting windows or shapes. Besides these geometric punches, you'll find an array of shaped punches of various sizes in the scrapbooking and paper sections of craft supply stores. You can fill your cardmaking toolbox with any number of these, including stars, hearts, and flowers.

Stamps

Rubber-stamp mania is still alive and well, and there are more stamp designs available on the market than ever. You can find a representation of just about anything that you want—from elephants to pansies. You can purchase stamps at a craft supply store, a stamp store, or on the Web. Hardware stores and some stamp stores carry metal stamps for stamping thin copper or other metal.

For decorating a series of cards, stamps are handy because you can replicate the image without much work. To slightly alter each replicated design, you can mix inks, or print only a portion of the stamp. Stamped images are often used in conjunction with collage, scrapbooking, or mixed media—techniques that are very popular among cardmakers. A set of alphabet stamps is great for adding messages to cards.

Heat Gun

This small blower heats air to a temperature that's safe for paper projects. You can use it to dry glues more quickly or emboss inks with embossing powders.

Eyelet Setting Tool

Eyelets function somewhat like grommets but are made up of a single piece instead of two pieces. You'll use the accompanying setting tool to roll down the backside of the eyelet to hold it in place.

Sewing Tools

You can hand- or machine-stitch paper cards to produce beautiful results. For stitching by hand, you'll need a sharp embroidery or tapestry needle for punching the holes before you insert the thread with a smaller needle. Doing this first clean punch in the paper will prevent tears and rough edges.

The possibilities for using a sewing machine to decorate cards are as varied as you can imagine. You can vary the colors of the thread, the stitches, and the overall patterns or designs you sew. Do something as simple as random stitching as a background effect, or embroider complex designs or names on the front of a card. Stitching on paper is really hot— and it's no wonder because it's loads of fun!

Supplies and Materials

The most basic stock supply of cardmaking is paper. After that, you'll need some glue. The rest of what you choose really depends on what you're making. Use this section to help sort things out and prioritize, because once you allow yourself to wander the aisles of your nearest craft supply store, you'll find a lot more things that will pique your imagination.

Adhesives

There are many choices for adhering paper or other decorative elements to your cards. You might find that you prefer one adhesive to another, but begin by buying a common white craft glue (PVA, or polyvinyl acetate) for general purposes. It's permanent, holds well, and dries clear. Glue sticks work well for adhering smaller pieces of material to a card. For tiny pieces, try out a glue pen, which allows you to trace a small amount of glue onto a very specific area.

All-purpose tacky craft glue is thick and dries clear. It works well for adding embellishments such as charms or wire. Spray adhesive prevents wrinkling and buckling if you're applying thin pieces of paper or fabric, and allows you to pull the material back off the card and reapply it without leaving a stain. If you use this adhesive, it's a good idea to place the pieces inside a cardboard box to prevent overspray on your work surface. Make sure to open a window when you use this adhesive because the fumes from it are strong.

Artist's acrylic medium, a longtime favorite of collage artists that dries hard and clear, is also a good choice for cards. It's thinner than craft glue and can be neatly applied with a paintbrush. It works well for attaching the parts of a collage or other small bits of material. If you wish, you can paint it on as a final layer on a collaged or altered piece. For fabric, there are also special glues on the market that can be purchased at fabric or craft supply stores.

Sponge and Cloths

It's a good idea to have a damp sponge on hand to wipe the glue off your hands while you're working on a project. If your hands are sticky, the glue can get transferred to your papers. Wipe your hands on a clean cotton cloth to remove the moisture before you begin working again.

Pens, Pencils, and Markers

Writing and drawing supplies will naturally find their way into your cardmaking arsenal. Besides sharp graphite pencils for marking, it's great to have a selection of colored pencils, pens, or markers that you can grab for adding lettering, simple drawings, or color. Many varieties of these writing and drawing implements are available. Try out various ones to find what you like best.

Artists' Paintbrushes

You'll find that small paintbrushes come in handy for adding watercolor washes or dabbing on paint to add color. Select some nice ones of a finer quality, and save the inexpensive brushes for applying glue, always keeping these two kinds of brushes separate.

Stamping Inks

There are lots of stamping inks available, and some work well for some things and some for others. For most purposes, you can use regular dye-based inks (the standard "office" inks) or pigment inks. These inks come in the form of inkpads that you can re-ink or in bottles from which you can ink a blank pad. The pads are either felt or foam. You'll find that dye-based inks usually come on felt pads, whereas pigment inks come on foam pads.

Dye-based inks work best on coated paper. Pigment inks are thicker inks that are opaque and slow to dry. They are more resistant to fading than dye-based ones. They work well on absorbent, uncoated paper (such as card stock). Because of their thickness, they are the ink of choice for embossing.

Embossing Powders

To create raised stamped surfaces, there are many embossing powders in various colors and even multicolor forms. These fine powders come in small jars. After you sprinkle the powder onto wet pigment inks, shake off the excess powder onto a piece of paper and return it to the jar. Then, use your heat gun to melt the powder and create a raised design. The first time you do this is magical—you'll be delighted with the beautiful effect that happens right before your eyes.

Mica Tiles

Compressed layers of translucent mica can be cut into particular shapes and layered on cards. You can stamp on the back or front of them, add press-type to them, or use them to cover photos to add a nostalgic look to a card. They are usually held in place with eyelets or brads.

Metal Accessories

You can add shine and visual interest to any card with copper wire or colored craft wire, copper sheets, or copper foil tape. You can also find bent-wire metal shapes in the scrapbooking section of a craft store that make interesting dimensional additions.

Brads and Eyelets

Brads, those used-to-be-merely-practical hardware items, now come in lots of shapes and colors. Use them as simple embellishments or to attach decorative papers or photographs to your cards. Eyelets are also very popular and can be used for the same purposes.

Beads

If you've ever been in a bead shop, you have a sense of how many types of beads there are on the market. These small glass dazzlers make a great addition to cards, whether stitched or glued in place. To add an elegant touch, stitch on small seed beads that come in a wide range of colors and finishes. Bugle beads are another good choice for stitching, and they can be nicely combined with seed beads. But don't limit yourself to these choices—experiment and have fun.

Threads

For hand stitching on cards, embroidery floss is a good choice and comes in many colors. Another option is sophisticated waxed linen. If you plan to machine-stitch cards, keep a stash of threads on hand to give yourself lots of choices. For sewing beads on cards, you'll need a spool or card of beading thread. The most common form, a single nylon strand, was originally developed for use with tapestries. These threads come in slightly different diameters or weights, so choose one that works well with your beads.

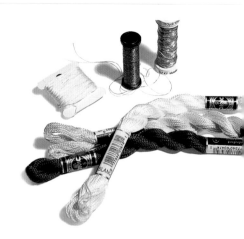

Found Objects and Natural Materials

Look around your home and yard, and you'll find an amazing amount of "stuff" that you can use to decorate cards. Found objects such as metal washers or buttons from your old sewing box can add visual interest to your design. Or what about watch parts, bits of costume jewelry, computer parts, or even tiny shards of broken glass? Natural materials such as butterfly wings, feathers, pressed flowers, and leaves make lovely additions too. Some of these materials now come prepackaged at craft stores, but it's always more satisfying to find your own and press them, if you have the time.

Scrapbooking Materials

If you're looking for an easy way to make a great impression without spending much time on a card, just head to the scrapbooking aisle of your local craft store! Because of the ever-escalating interest in this activity, there are now entire aisles devoted to it. Hanging on those many pegs are items that will imbue your cards with instant pizzazz. Besides the many scrapbooking papers, you'll find miniatures, or tiny three-dimensional accessories. These tiny trinkets are especially great for special occasion cards.

From baby shoes to soccer balls, you'll find something that fits your theme.

Another great find are stamps and stickers (both text and images), which make it so easy to make a card look professional. Tiny flowers, butterflies, hearts, and other shapes lend instant dimension to your project. Small stickers in the shape of frames are fun to work with because you can place images or text inside of them. And don't overlook colorful stick-on dots as an option. In addition, there's always a delightful array of stick-on alphabets. You can mix and match lettering or use elegant, refined versions—whichever fits your purposes.

Techniques

This section tells you how to make your own blank cards before you get to the really interesting stuff—decorating and embellishing them! Techniques are just ways of doing things that have worked for others, but that doesn't mean that you can't make up your own or even improve upon the ideas. By all means, don't always follow the rules. If you allow your artsy side to guide your dexterous one, you'll not only get better results, but you'll have more fun. Artfully combining techniques can lead to wonderful discoveries.

Cutting, Scoring, and Folding a Blank Card

You may find an amazing paper that you want to make into a blank card, or simply want to save money by cutting and folding your own cards. Or perhaps you'd like to make a card with an unusual fold. Making your own cards is very simple with some basic equipment and a bit of patience.

✿ When you decide on the size that you want, use a paper trimmer or a craft knife and cutting mat to neatly trim a piece of card stock or other paper to twice the size of one panel. In other words, you'll double the width of the paper in the direction of the fold. So, if you want to make a 4 x 5-inch card, cut a piece of paper that is 8 x 5 inches. If you plan to insert your card in a

premade envelope, the folded card should be approximately ⅛ to ⅜ inch smaller than the envelope so it slides in easily. If you're planning to make a thicker card with added embellishment, take this into account when cutting the card. You'll need to make the card even smaller to fit it into the envelope.

✿ On the side of the paper that will fall inside your card, mark a line with a light pencil mark along the fold line. Place your ruler along this line and score the line with the pointed end of the bone folder. Doing this breaks the top fibers in the paper so the paper will fold crisply.

✿ Fold the card along the line you scored. Beginning at the top of the card, press the edge of the card with the curved portion of the bone folder to make a neat fold, and you're ready to go!

Gluing and Burnishing Flat Pieces

To apply any flat piece of material to a card, you'll need to keep a few things in mind. It's important to pay attention to this part of making a card so that everything stays stuck to your card and doesn't fall off later on.

✿ Place the material you plan to adhere wrong side up on a scrap of paper. This is the side you'll adhere. Next comes the important part. Apply an even coat of adhesive over the entire surface, being sure to extend past the edges. When you're done, pick up the piece with the tip of your finger or the end of a craft knife and position it on the card.

⚙ Now place a piece of blank paper or wax paper over the piece to protect it while you burnish the whole area with your bone folder. Wax paper is a great choice because it allows you to see what you're doing.

⚙ When you're finished adding pieces to the card, you can press it underneath a pile of books for maximum adhesion.

Decorating and Embellishing Your Card

Now comes the fun part! Designing and decorating your cards can be incredibly satisfying. The previous sections about cardmaking materials and tools have already introduced you to some technique-related information. This section summarizes some of the most popular approaches used in cardmaking today.

There are really no rules or restrictions and the possibilities for dressing up your small blank canvases are truly endless. The projects that follow this section show lots of variations of these techniques and more, giving you plenty of inspiration as you pursue your own individual expression.

COLLAGE AND MIXED MEDIA

Collage and mixed media—techniques whose names were once somewhat exclusive "art speak"—have now been fully adopted and adapted by crafters. The initial development of collage as an art form is credited to Pablo Picasso (1881-1973) and Georges Braque (1882-1963), and now, many years later, it is a major trend. Collage and mixed media go hand-in-hand.

The term mixed media grew out of the idea of combining media, instead of being limited to one, as was the tradition of old-school painting or drawing. Several decades ago, mixed media was considered to be somewhat rebellious and avant garde! Today, it is a catchall term for using many media in one piece.

These techniques are such a fit for cards that it's no surprise they're so popular. Collage, in its most basic form, is simply cutting and pasting materials together to create an interesting surface. One of the engaging things about collage is that it is a process-oriented technique. This simply means that you can make it up as you go along! Gather your materials from a variety of sources (papers, cardboards, fabric, or other materials of your choice) and cut, tear, rip, and paste to your heart's content. Of course, if you like a more planned, less improvisational approach, you can plan and then scrutinize your design before you actually adhere the pieces, moving them around to see how things play off of one another.

From this simple concept of layering and recontextualizing things to make a new and unique design, the sky's the limit! Add watercolor washes, additional color with markers or pens, drawn or scribbled lines with pens or colored pencils, and you'll begin to get the idea. This activity can really be fun and freeing. And if you are feeling timid, you don't feel pressure to begin on a blank card. Just play around with ideas on some scrap paper. Do some little sketches first.

Collage and mixed media truly are art forms, and along with these endeavors comes a lot of impromptu decision-making and exploration. Many of the projects in this book use these techniques and demonstrate some of the tricks of the trade that you can apply to make fascinating and artistic cards.

SCRAPBOOKING

The scrapbooking industry has given birth to a virtual cornucopia of creative possibilities for cardmaking. The personal approach of displaying photos and memorabilia is what makes scrapbooking so appealing. In addition, it's a craft that virtually anyone can do.

Think of it as an extension of collage and mixed media.

To apply the idea of scrapbooking to cards, simply add embellishments to dress up the front of a card and make it special. Small miniatures, stickers, wire, ribbon, pressed flowers, and, of course, scrapbooking papers, are just a few of the many materials from which to choose.

STAMPING

Take your pick from the huge world of stamps, and add designs, shapes, or lettering to cards. The stamped images can serve as your only decoration or be added to collage or mixed media. Add beading or embellishment to a simple stamped design to make it elegant. An alphabet of stamps is handy

for adding greetings, text, names, or messages. Pick and choose from various fonts.

Use embossing powders if you want to add dimension to your inked designs. Don't be afraid to experiment. Remember, the stamp is only the tool, and you're the artist.

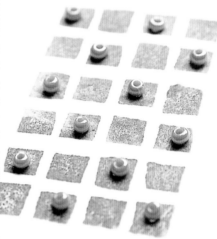

STITCHING AND BEADING

Stitching on cards can produce impressive results without a lot of work. You can hand stitch cards with embroidery threads, waxed linen, or other heavier threads. This kind of stitching bears the mark of your hand and will no doubt make your card a keepsake.

To work more quickly and create more complex designs, use machine stitching. You have almost unlimited possibilities for stitching since you can change them and mix them up.

You can create almost any design with thread, just as you would with pens, pencils, or paints. The stitching can be purely decorative (similar to embroidery) or it can serve to hold parts of cards together (such as layered sections). The palette of threads available is as wide as the world of fabrics, so you should have no trouble finding what you want.

If you're already using threads, you might as well add beads. Use beading thread to attach the beads. Seed beads make a great choice because of their variety of color and size. Punch holes with the beading needle before sewing the beads in place.

MAKING POP-UPS

Pop-up cards are three-dimensional. They might contain elements that pop up when you open up the card, or open out into attractive freestanding pieces. Sometimes they have elements that slide in and out of the picture when you pull the sides of them.

Pop-ups often aren't as complicated as they look, but they do require patience, a sharp cutting blade, and a steady hand. To make them, you'll cut paper parts that fold and fit together to make the final construction. One thing is certain, these amazing cards make an impression!

card
projects

The following pages are full of creative, fun, and artistic cards
made with lots of different techniques. Many of the projects
include variations, showing you how simple it is to take an idea,
slightly alter it, and really make it your own.

materials

Cards and matching envelopes

Scraps of collected fabric

Colored pencils or paints (optional)

tools

Fabric scissors

Decorative-edged scissors (optional)

Fabric glue

Heavy book

Fabulous Fabric Cards

These charming cards show off the inventive eye of the designer. Try out unusual combinations of color and pattern to achieve your own eye-catching results.

process

1 Choose several fabrics for decorating the front of your card.

2 Cut out bits and pieces, and experiment with various backgrounds and combinations. Combine different textures and patterns to create contrast. If you wish, use decorative-edged scissors to create different edges.

3 Layer your fabrics and adhere them to the card with fabric glue.

4 If you wish, use colored media, such as pencils or paints, to add bits of color to the fabric. Allow any paint to dry.

5 Press the card underneath a heavy book so that it dries flat.

Altered CD Cards

Use old CDs as the substrate for a whimsical collaged card.
The plastic container makes a handy envelope for your fanciful work of art.

materials

Used CDs and cases

Decorative papers for the background

Acrylic medium, white craft glue, or glue stick

Collage materials such as magazine or newspaper clippings, pages from old books, photographs, or postage stamps

Trims, buttons, copper foil tape, and other decorative additions

Rubber alphabet stamps and inkpad (optional)

Metal letter stamps for embossing copper foil (optional)

Waxed linen cord for hangers

Beads for hangers

tools

Toothpicks, craft sticks, or small paintbrush for applying adhesive

Craft knife and cutting mat

Decorative-edged scissors

Small handheld drill

process

1 Apply a thin coat of adhesive to one side of the CD and lay it flat on decorative paper, smooth it out, and let it dry. When it's thoroughly dry, use the craft knife to trim the paper from around the CD. Adhere paper to the other side of the CD too.

2 If you wish, trim the paper around the hole in the CD on one side only, leaving the other side covered. This creates a little well for holding embellishments, such as buttons.

3 For your collage, clip out bits of text that fit your theme from old newspapers, magazines, or books. Select some appropriate images to go with your words, and cut them from magazines, old photos, or books.

4 Arrange the pieces of your collage on the front and adhere them after you decide on the design. Add buttons or trinkets to fill up the small well in the center of the CD.

5 Use the round shape of the CD to your advantage, arranging the pieces of your collage with this overall shape in mind. For instance, curve your lettering or angle your images so that they relate well to the curved edges.

6 If you wish, add stamped lettering as well. You can stamp words on paper and collage them to your CD or stamp the lettering directly on the design. Add more subtle messages with stamped copper foil.

7 To add a cord for hanging the CD, drill a hole near the edge of it. Through the hole, make a loop with the waxed linen cord and tie it off close to the edge of the CD before adding decorative beads to the cord and tying them off to secure them.

8 Place the CD in the accompanying plastic case, which serves as your envelope.

Lovely Layered Cards

These cards can be made with any sturdy scrapbooking paper
and die-cut embellishments that are layered to create a playful effect.

materials

Sheet of faux-finish scrapbooking paper, 6 x 12 inches

Sheet of coordinating scrapbooking paper, 6 x 10¾ inches

Piece of coordinating paper for layered flower design, about 4 x 4 inches

Waxed linen in color that coordinates with top layer paper, about 6 inches

Die-cut leather or paper shape

White craft glue

Metal eyelets or brads

tools

Bone folder

Ruler

Cutting mat

Awl

Sewing needle for waxed linen

Large shape punch in shape of your choice that is larger in dimension than your die-cut shapes

Punching mat or stack of magazines

Eyelet-setting tool (optional)

Small hammer (optional)

Glue brush

Sheet of wax paper

process

1 Fold the piece of faux-finish paper in half widthwise. Use the bone folder to score it along the fold line and crease it.

2 Place the top layer of coordinating scrapbooking paper in front of you horizontally. Use the ruler to measure in 6 inches from one of the short sides, and lightly mark a fold line. Use the bone folder to score and press the fold.

3 Place the cutting mat on your table. On top of this surface, open out both of the folded papers. Place the faux-finish paper facedown. Stack the shorter piece of paper on top of it.

4 Use a pencil to mark the center point of the fold lightly. Make a mark 1 inch from either side of this center point along the fold line. Use the awl to carefully punch through all three marks and both sheets of paper.

5 Sew the two sheets together. To begin, thread the needle with waxed linen and push it through the center hole from the inside of the card. Push the needle through one of the side holes, back to the inside of the card. Then push the needle back through the center hole before pushing it down through the remaining side hole. Push the needle back through the center hole. Knot the thread inside the card, and trim it.

6 To embellish the front of the card, use a craft punch and the remaining piece of paper to cut out a shape. Glue the die-cut shape in the center of the larger shape. Let the glue dry.

7 Place the composite shape faceup on a punching mat or stack of magazines. Use the awl to punch a hole in the center of the shape. Use the eyelet tool and hammer to set an eyelet or push a brad through the hole.

8 Flip the shape over and block half of the back of it with a sheet of paper. Brush a thin layer of glue onto the exposed half.

9 With the card faceup, place the wax paper between the two paper layers on the front of the card. Adhere the shape to the front of the card, allowing the unglued half to hang over the second layer. Let it dry with the wax paper in place.

Variation: Use a square-shaped punch to create a window in the top layer of the card. Glue the die-cut shape with decorative center eyelet or brad on the second layer of the card, inside the window.

Stamped & Beaded Cards

The understated elegance of these cards and matching envelopes
makes them a tasteful option for any occasion.

materials

Blank white cards and envelopes

Geometric patterned rubber stamps

Inkpads and colored inks

Beading thread

Seed beads

tools

Beading needle

Scissors

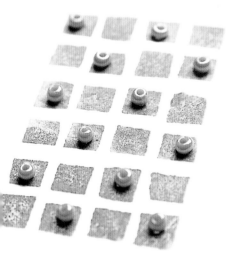

process

1 Stamp the front of your card. If you wish, create a blended look by applying several colors of ink on the stamp. Set it aside to dry.

2 Use a beading needle to poke holes through the surface of the stamped design in a pattern of your choice. You can use the stamp design as a guideline or simply follow its contours.

3 Thread the needle with about 12 inches of beading thread. From the backside, guide the needle through one of the holes. Knot the end and cut off the excess thread.

4 Place a single seed bead on the needle, then guide the needle back through the hole it came out of. Bring the needle back up through another hole, add a bead, and then go back through that same hole. Repeat until all the holes have been filled with beads.

5 Knot the remaining thread inside the card.

6 Repeat with related stamps and beading to make a set of coordinating cards.

7 Repeat the same decorating process on the flap of a matching envelope. To vary the design, cover a portion of the stamp with paper to create a similar, but smaller pattern.

Touch of Nature Cards

The idea for this card grew out of the designer's attraction to blank green cards.
He layered dried plant materials with other materials to produce elegant results.

materials

Card stock and business-sized envelopes

Card template (see page 138)

Patterned tissue paper (for the punched card)

Vellum (for the punched card)

Neutral ribbon printed with words (available at craft supply stores)

Skeleton leaves, dried ferns, pressed flowers, or other dried natural materials

Glue stick

tools

Craft knife and cutting mat

2-inch circular hole punch (for the punched card)

Scissors

process

1 Use the enlarged template as a guide to cut the card stock. Punch the holes with the circular hole punch as shown. Fold the card as indicated.

2 Use the hole punch to punch out two pieces of the patterned tissue paper and the vellum for each cut hole.

3 With the card folded, mark the placement of the circular holes with a light pencil line inside the card. Open out the card and glue the patterned tissue paper within these circles. Layer the vellum on top, smoothing it out. Allow the papers to dry.

4 Close the card and cut pieces of ribbon to fit the length of the card. Adhere them to the front underneath the circular windows.

5 Glue trimmed natural materials inside the circular windows on top of the layered papers. You can either repeat the same shape or vary the materials.

Variation: To make a simpler card without punched windows and layered papers, attach decorative ribbons and natural materials, using the horizontal format as your guide.

LOVE IN A PUFF
RGANICALLY GROWN FLOWER SEEDS

Seed Packet Cards

An envelope of translucent paper vellum allows hints of its contents to show through. These triangular cards contain seeds and directions for planting them—wonderful tokens to hand to friends at a spring garden party.

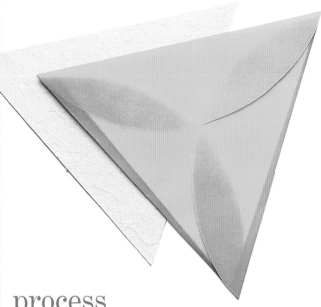

materials

Template (page 139)

Light green vellum

Sheet of card stock

Sheet of text paper

Package of seeds

Photocopy of seed package or other related images or clip art

tools

Scissors

Adjustable circle cutter (optional)

Bone folder

Metal ruler

White craft glue or glue stick

Computer (optional)

Photocopy machine (optional)

process

1 If you're not using a circle cutter, enlarge the template shown so that the circle is about 5 inches in diameter.

2 Lay the vellum on top of it and trace the circle on it. Carefully cut out the circular shape with a pair of sharp scissors.

Note: If you have a circle cutter, skip this step, and use it to cut out a 5-inch circular shape.

3 Using the template as a guide, fold the flaps in one at a time to form a neat triangular envelope. Reinforce the creases with a bone folder.

4 From the card stock, cut out an insert triangle of the size indicated on the template.

5 Use your ruler to draw a slightly smaller triangle on text-weight paper. Extract images and text from your photocopy for the front enclosure and paste them into the triangular shape, or scan clip art and arrange your own type and graphics on a computer so that they fit the shape. Once this master copy is prepared, make a photocopy of it. Cut out this piece and glue it to the card-stock triangle.

6 Within the same triangular format, type up directions for planting the seeds on your computer and print them out. Cut out the shape and glue it to the other side of the cardstock triangle.

Variation: If you're not computer savvy, or just prefer a more handmade look, simply grab a nice pen and write your message and directions on the insert. You can spice it up with colored media or collaged images.

Stamped and Embossed Tri-Fold Cards

These impressive-looking cards are extremely easy to make and replicate.
Keep a stack on hand for dashing off thoughtful notes.

materials

Large sheet of neutral-colored
card stock

Sheet of white card stock

Rubber stamps in floral designs or
other designs of your choice

Embossing ink and powder

tools

Craft knife and cutting mat

Metal ruler or small T-square

Paper cutter (optional)

Bone folder

Heat gun

process

1 Use a craft knife or paper cutter to trim one $15\frac{3}{4}$ x $7\frac{1}{4}$-inch piece from the neutral card stock. Fold the paper in thirds, making the first two panels about $5\frac{1}{4}$ inches, and the final panel slightly narrower, so it can fold to the card's inside. Smooth the edges with a bone folder to create a tri-fold card.

2 Open out the card, and use the craft knife to cut a $\frac{3}{4}$ x $4\frac{1}{2}$-inch window in the center of the middle panel. A small T-square comes in handy for making straight angles.

3 Cut a $4\frac{1}{2}$ x $5\frac{3}{4}$-inch rectangular piece from the white card stock. Stamp an image onto the paper and immediately cover it with embossing powder, before the ink has a chance to dry. Cover all of the stamped area and shake off the excess powder. Use the heat gun to activate (melt) the embossing powder.

4 Once the stamped piece has dried, place it behind the window. Keeping the piece in position, open out the card and lightly mark the upper right and lower left corner on the first panel. Use your craft knife to cut across these lines diagonally to make two slits to hold the card. Insert the image and close the card.

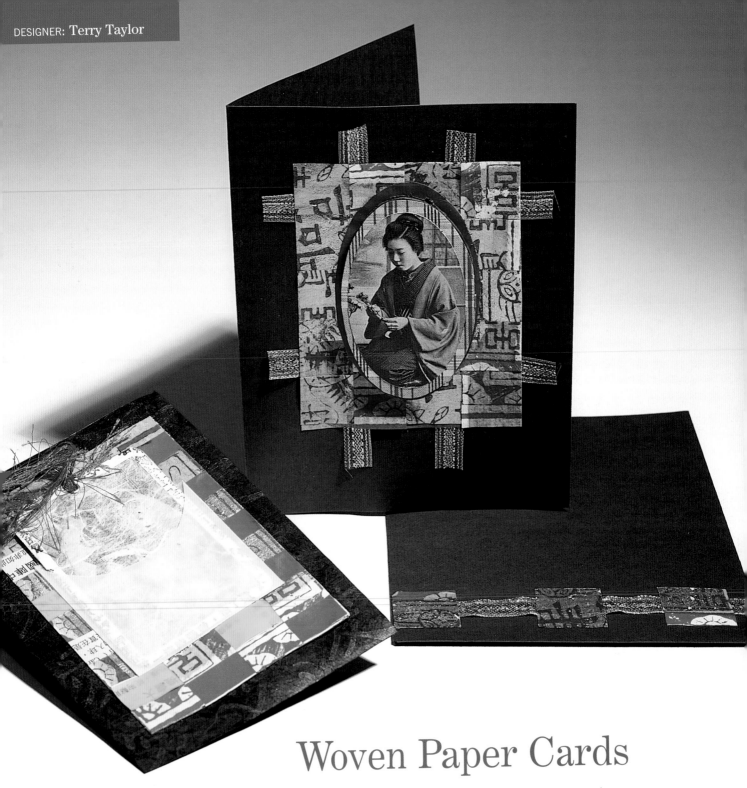

Woven Paper Cards

On these fashionable cards, a background of woven joss papers, chopstick wrappers, and Oriental newsprint make an intriguing ground for other decorative elements. The weaving looks impressive but is easy to do.

materials

Joss papers or other Asian-themed decorative papers

Low-tack masking tape

Bold and red striped ribbon and chopstick wrappers (optional)

Acrylic medium

Black cards and envelopes

Embellishments such as stamped and embossed mica tiles (see page 16), altered tags, collaged playing cards, color copies of photographs or postcards, chopstick wrappers with printed messages

tools

Craft knife, scissors, or paper cutter

Paintbrush

Wax paper

Heavy book

process

1 Use a craft knife, scissors, or paper cutter to cut decorative papers into strips about ½ inch wide.

2 On a flat surface, place four to six strips close together. Use a length of low-tack masking tape to hold the strips in place.

3 Weave additional paper strips over and under the taped strips, adjusting the position of each strip as you weave so they're close together. You can also weave in ribbon or chopstick wrappers to lend variety to the design.

4 When you've finished weaving, secure all the ends of the woven paper pieces by brushing on a very light coat of acrylic medium. Cover the weaving with wax paper, and place a heavy book on top until the medium dries.

5 Remove the book and wax paper. Trim the ends of the weaving. If needed, brush additional acrylic medium on the ends to secure them.

6 Adhere the woven paper to a card as a background for collage and additional embellishments of your choice.

Layered Paper and Metal Cards

Use subtle combinations of materials to make these simple but sophisticated cards.
Add a dimensional embellishment to create a focal point.

materials

Off-white handmade paper (available
at art supply stores)

Beige or black background paper

Flat metallic materials for layering:
copper or brass wire mesh; leaf or
foil in gold, platinum, or silver

Card stock (optional)

Copper-colored thread (optional)

Polymer clay cane slices (available at
craft supply stores) or other dimensional embellishments

Gold or silver fabric paint (optional)

tools

Bone folder

Metal ruler

Scissors or craft knife and
cutting mat

White craft glue or glue stick

Tacky glue

Embroidery needle or other sharp
needle (optional)

process

1 Decide on the size of your
card, and cut or tear a piece of
handmade paper to the dimensions you need. Fold the card over,
and use the bone folder to crease
the fold.

2 Cut pieces of mesh, leaf, or
foil to layer on the front of your
card. Cut a smaller piece of contrasting paper to place on top of
the background. After you've
decided on size and placement,
glue the materials in place on the
front of the card.

3 Add a final dimensional
embellishment on top of the layered design, and attach it with a
dab of tacky glue.

Variation: Place torn pieces of
handmade paper together on the
front of a piece of card stock so
they meet and form a seam. If you
wish, add a decorative piece of
paper, a dried leaf, or other decorative accent along the seam. Glue
the pieces down and let them dry.
Thread the needle with copper-
colored thread and stitch the seam
from top to bottom. Layer pieces of
paper and other embellishments on
another section of the card. If you
wish, add a splash of gold or silver
fabric paint to the design.

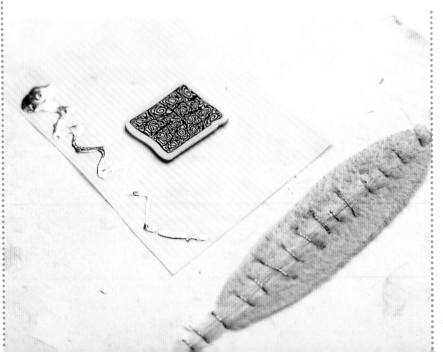

Altered Tin Book Card

Expand your idea of what a greeting card can be by using a flat tin
as the "envelope" for your message. Assemble collaged pages to make an intriguing
visual enclosure. This designer documented a trip to Paris taken with a friend.

materials

Flat tin (such as an old candy tin)

Spray paint

Decorative tissue paper or other patterned paper

Acrylic medium

Metal lettering

Photos and memorabilia

Scrapbook embellishments

Card stock

Decorative brad (for holding the pages together)

Fabric or woven envelope (optional)

tools

Sanding sponge

Scissors

Paintbrush

Measuring tape

Photocopy machine

Hole punch

process

1. Abrade the surface of the tin with a sanding sponge so that it can be coated with paint. Place the tin flat on newspapers and spray it with a coat of paint to give it a solid base color. Allow both parts to dry.

2. Cut a piece of tissue paper to fit the lid of the tin. Use acrylic medium to adhere the paper, smoothing it as you go. Let it dry and then paint the tissue with another coat of medium.

3. Collage images of your choice onto the lid of the tin. Attach dimensional metal lettering and other embellishments to complete your message and design.

4. Measure the tin's interior and cut several pieces of card stock to fit inside it. See how many will stack inside without being too tight. Make sure you can close the lid and allow a bit of extra room for the brad fastener.

5. Based roughly on the size of the interior, create combined photocopied collage images using memorabilia such as photographs, clippings, maps, receipts, or postcards. To do this, arrange the items facedown on the copier and reduce them. Create as many collage images as needed for your insert.

6. Use acrylic medium to adhere the photocopied images to the card stock pieces. Add other images, memorabilia, or scrapbooking embellishments. If desired, you can write remembrances on the reverse of the pages.

7. Punch a hole in the top corner of each card stock page and use the brad to hold the pages together.

Autumnal Cards and Tags

The compatible textures and coloration of fall leaves, artistic papers, and frayed fringes lend these beautiful cards and tags a nostalgic look that captures autumn's bittersweet nature.

materials

Autumn leaves (reds or dark yellows)

Wax paper

Large book

Acrylic gel medium

Rubber stamp for embossed design

Embossing inks

Cards and envelopes in neutrals or
    subtle colors

Regular-sized and mini-tags

Decorative papers

Decorative ribbons or fringe

tools

Paintbrush

Heat gun

process

1 Collect fall leaves and press them in wax paper between the pages of a large book.

2 After the leaves have dried but still retain their color, paint on acrylic gel medium to varnish them.

3 To create a beautiful effect, stamp and emboss the leaves. Be careful not to get too close to the leaf when using the heat gun, so you don't burn it.

4 Stamp the tags. Tear pieces of paper to create a frayed and natural-looking edge.

5 If you wish, emboss a colored piece of paper with a patterned design, and cut out that design element to use on a card along with a leaf.

6 Layer the papers and leaves as you wish on the tags and cards to create interesting designs. Glue each piece into place, smoothing it as you go.

7 If you wish, thread decorative fringe through the tags for a final touch.

8 On each envelope, use one of the rubber stamps to add a decorative touch.

Beautiful Paper Fan Card

This artist accidentally discovered an interesting paper technique when teaching
a children's art class many years ago. Simply paint washes of color on paper,
and use the "scrunching" trick described here to get great effects!

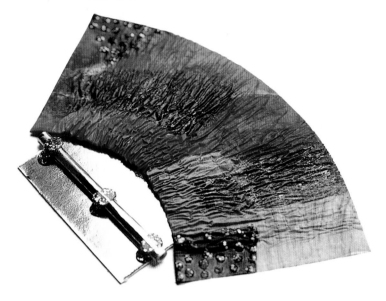

materials

Cards and matching envelopes

White vellum or other thin but
  stiff paper

Watercolors

Wax crayons (optional)

Pencil

White craft glue

Glitter

Thin gold mat board

Narrow wooden dowel or
  cooking skewer

Gold foil

Gold fabric paint

tools

Scissors or craft knife and
  cutting mat

Glue brush

process

1 Paint random streaks of watercolor on the white paper, allowing the colors to run and mix together. If you wish, add more color and draw lines on top with wax crayons. Let the paper dry.

2 Cut a strip of the paper about 3 inches wide from the painted paper. Roll the paper on the pencil and then scrunch it into a tube shape. Remove the paper from the pencil and unfold it. Paint some glue on the surface of the paper and add bits of glitter.

3 Fold under the bottom edge of the paper and bend it into a fan-like shape. Trim the top edge if needed. Cut a piece of thin gold mat board about 1½ inches square to fit underneath the paper fan. Set these pieces aside.

4 Apply adhesive to several inches of the end of the wooden dowel or skewer and let it dry slightly until tacky. Roll gold foil onto the glued area and trim the foil as needed. Allow the covered dowel or skewer to dry.

5 Use scissors or a craft knife to cut a piece of the wooden dowel or skewer to a length that slightly overlaps the gold mat board piece.

6 Glue the gold square slightly below center on the card. Layer the fan over it so that it overlaps about half of it. Glue the fan in place without smoothing it out, so that it is textured.

7 Use three drips of gold fabric paint to attach the foiled wooden piece underneath the fan to the gold square. Allow the paint to dry thoroughly.

8 Use the pencil to scribe your artistic signature beneath the piece, if you wish. Now your card is suitable for framing!

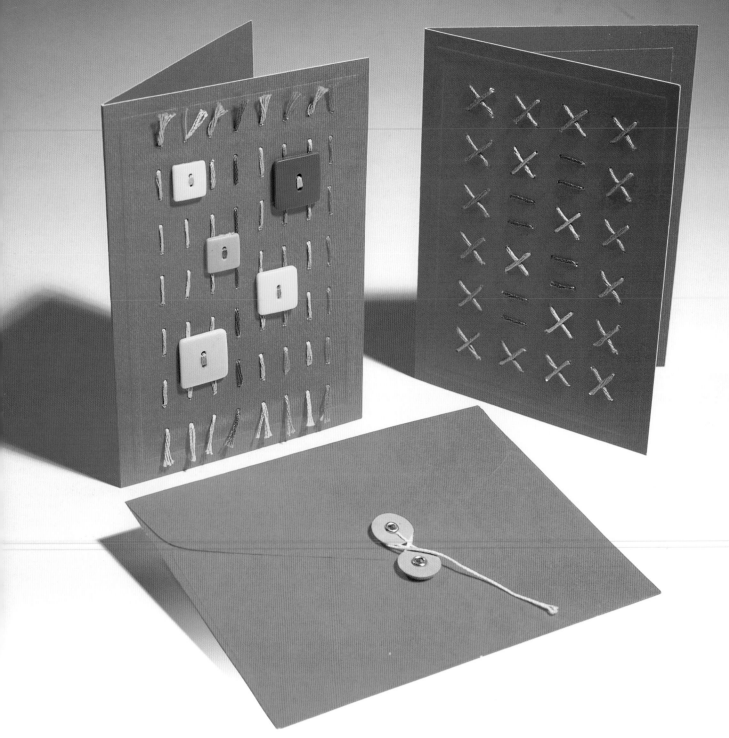

Hip Stitched Cards

Use colorful cards and bright embroidery floss to create
one-of-a-kind cards that show off your handiwork.

materials

Colored cards (heavy stock) and matching envelopes

Embroidery floss in contrasting colors

Clear cellophane tape (optional)

Buttons or embellishments (optional)

Colored paper for insert

White craft glue or glue stick

Round fasteners with grommets and string closure for envelopes

tools

Sharp scissors

Ruler

Sharp pencil

Awl or sharp needle

Tapestry needle

process

1 Create a simple grid on the front of several cards by using a ruler and pencil to mark a vertical row of equally spaced points down each side of the card. Turn the ruler so that it is horizontal, and mark equally spaced rows across the card, connecting your vertical points.

2 On the front of each card, carefully pierce each of the holes with an awl or a sharp needle.

3 Thread a tapestry needle with a length of embroidery floss. Begin by stitching the simplest design, the one that shows thread running down the card in vertical rows. Push the needle down into the first hole and come back out through the second hole, moving the thread in and out until you reach the other side. When you're done, pull the thread tight and trim both ends so they're clean.

4 Try other stitching combinations (as shown in the variation) using the exact same punched grid. Use your imagination—there are lots of possibilities. When creating a more complicated design, you can tie off the threads inside the card as you work, or you can use clear cellophane tape to hold the ends in place after you cut them.

5 If you wish, use colorful thread to sew on buttons or other embellishments to complement your stitching.

6 To cover tied off stitches inside the card, cut out an insert from paper and glue it in place.

7 Add round decorative fasteners to the outside of your envelopes, tying the whole design together.

Recycled Stitched Cards

This designer enjoys recycling bits of leftover papers and fabrics that are too beautiful to throw away. Using such materials adds to the handmade look of each card.

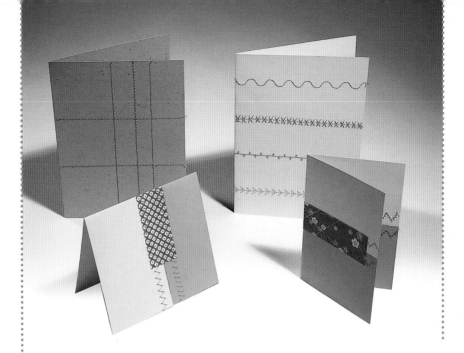

materials

Scrap sheets of card stock

Sewing threads

Old cards or postcards (optional)

Scraps of decorative paper or fabrics

Glue stick

tools

Bone folder

Scissors or craft knife and cutting mat

Sewing machine

Decorative flower hole punches (optional)

process

1 To make cards sewn with various stitches as the only decoration, trim and fold a card from card stock. Then sew a design of pattern and color on the front of the card that's made up of different stitches and threads. The "less is more" approach of these beautiful cards is what makes them so lovely.

2 Another idea is to decorate the front panel of the card with part of an old card. Just cut it to size and stitch around the edges to hold it in place, and you're done.

3 To use nice pieces of paper that aren't large enough for a single card, cut two paper strips that fit together to form a larger card, and cut a piece of decorative paper or fabric to layer on top of the strips where they join together. Then sew lines of decorative stitching on top of the decorative inset, above and below the line where the papers join.

4 To decorate your card with paper or fabric flowers, punch out paper shapes with decorative hole punches or cut out the flower shapes from bits of fabric. Place them on the card, layering them if you like, and tack them in place with glue. Draw a light pencil line from the flower to indicate a stem, and cut out leaves from decorative paper. Glue them in place along the stem. After the glue dries, stitch from the center of the flower to the bottom of the stem, crossing over the leaves. Erase any pencil marks.

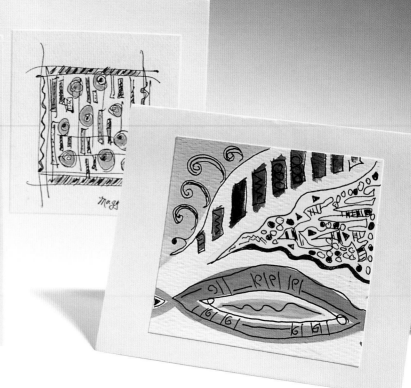

Doodle Cards

Random drawings, scribbled while you're on the phone
or in a meeting, can be transformed into playful cards!

materials

Blank cards and matching
  envelopes

Drawing paper or heavy text paper

Fine-tip black pen or other nice
  drawing pen

Glue stick

Colored media such as colored gel
  pens, markers, or watercolors

tools

Photocopy machine

Scissors or craft knife

process

1. Gather favorite doodles from scrap papers or notebook pages or create new ones on heavy paper with a black pen. (It's a great idea to carry a doodling notebook with you at all times for those unforeseen opportunities!)

2. Use a photocopy machine to enlarge or reduce your doodles. Cut them up and arrange them into new composite designs.

3. Use a glue stick to attach the doodled parts to paper. Make several photocopies of the designs.

Cut out areas from the photocopied designs in sizes that fit the cards and allow a nice white border. Glue each design to the front of a card, and press them underneath a heavy book while they dry.

4. Use colored media to add color to each copied design. If you wish, you can make a series of multiples from the same design and alter the cards by simply changing the colors you use on each.

materials

Sheets of colored corrugated paper

Colored envelopes

White craft glue

Matching text paper for card insert

Decorative brads (optional)

tools

Large shape punches

Craft knife or scissors

Smaller shape punches (optional)

Corrugated Marquetry Cards

These cheerful cards are made with decorative
inlays of simple corrugated paper.

process

1 Experiment with the large paper punches to figure out how to position them and best use them to your advantage. Save the shapes that you cut out because you might want to use them later.

2 Use the craft knife or scissors to cut the corrugated paper to double the height of the finished piece. Fold it over to form a card. Punch out large shapes of your choice along the length of the card, leaving open windows.

3 Punch the same shapes from a contrasting color of corrugated paper. Fit the shapes into the negative spaces.

4 You can make your design more complex by punching smaller shapes out of the larger ones. Fit these into contrasting windows formed by removing them.

5 Hold all the pieces in place by backing them with adhered text paper.

6 If you wish, layer the shapes with smaller, punched shapes attached with decorative brads.

Flower Power Cards

These fun cards will bring a smile to anyone's lips. Stamped and embossed
mica tile is used to update a retro theme.

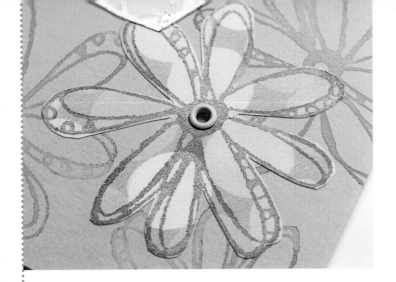

materials

Brightly colored card stock

Vellum envelopes

Sheets of mica tile

Pigment stamp pad

Rubber stamp with design of
   your choice (for mica tile)

Embossing powder

Sheet of decorative paper

Rubber stamp with daisy design

Dye-based stamp pad

Eyelets

Sheet of colored paper

Brads (optional)

tools

Craft knife and cutting mat

Bone folder

Heat gun

Glue stick

Small hammer

Awl

Eyelet-setting tool

Large shape punch

process

1 Cut the card stock to fit the dimensions of the vellum envelopes. Fold each card that you plan to decorate, and crease it with a bone folder.

2 Separate out as many sheets of mica tile as you need.

3 Think about the shape of the stamped image when you cut the mica. If you wish, you can stamp the image onto a piece of paper and place it behind the mica to see how it looks.

4 Load your stamp with pigment ink and stamp it on the back of the mica tile. Sprinkle embossing powder on the stamped image and apply heat with a heat gun to dry it.

5 To make the card shown in the foreground, use the flower stamp and dye-based pad to randomly stamp the decorative paper as well as the front of the card. Cut out the stamped images and use a glue stick to adhere them to the front of the card. Overlap the cutout decorative flowers on top of the stamped flowers to produce a sense of depth or foreground and background.

6 Punch holes with the awl in the center of the flowers, and set eyelets in them.

7 Use the large shape punch to punch out a simple shape from the piece of colored paper. Glue it in the center of the card. Position the embossed mica over the card stock shape, and attach it to the card with eyelets.

Variation: Attach a stamped and embossed image on mica to a pre-printed, purchased card with decorative brads instead of eyelets.

Flowering Love Cards

These unquestionably original cards combine common materials such
as paper bags, construction and graph paper, and small cupcake papers.

materials

Large paper bag (a grocery bag works well)

Colored construction paper

Cupcake papers

Graph or notebook paper (for your message inside)

Old photographs (originals, photocopies, or scanned and printed)

Colored thread of your choice

White glue or glue stick

Small box for envelope

tools

Scissors

Metal ruler

Craft knife

Sewing machine

Stamps in press-type style (for message inside)

process

❶ Use scissors to cut open the paper bag, and lay the paper flat on your work surface. Use a ruler to outline the edges of your cards on the paper. Remember to double the width of the paper. Cut out the cards and fold them in half to give them a crease line.

❷ Open the cards back out so they're flat. Use scissors to cut out circles from construction paper to serve as the background for each of your flower designs. As another option, cut out a piece of rectangular background paper, as shown on the smaller card, and then cut out a circle from it with the craft knife so that the brown paper card shows behind it.

❸ Place the background pieces on the front panel of the card. Decide on the facial images you want to use for the center of each flower. If needed, size the images so they fit inside your cupcake papers. Print them out on heavier weight paper so that the images are stiff.

❹ Cut these center images slightly larger than the circular bottom of each cupcake paper so that the papers will be pushed out slightly after you glue the photos in place. Place the faces inside the cupcake papers on top of the circles to see how everything looks.

❺ Once you've decided on the positioning of these key pieces, draw a light pencil line to indicate the stems of the flowers, and set aside the background pieces, cupcake papers, and facial images.

❻ Cut or tear a piece of graph or notebook paper to go inside the card with your message on it. Use the lettering stamps to print a message on the paper. Glue the paper inside the card. Let the glue dry thoroughly before you begin any stitching.

7 With the card faceup and open, stitch around the edges with brightly colored thread. Stitch a stem pattern that connects to the flowers. Then flip the whole card over and stitch a design around your message if you wish.

8 After you've finished stitching, retrieve your cut pieces to glue them down on the front as planned. Glue down the background pieces and, on top, the photos inside the cupcake papers.

9 Cut leaves out from other photos, and glue them in place along the stitched stems. (Eyes peering from leaves make an intriguing design!)

10 If you wish, decorate the inside with more cutout flower designs, lettering, and stiching.

11 Use a small paper box as an envelope for your dimensional card.

materials

Heavy paper

Cards and matching envelopes

Color photocopies of found materials from nature walks such as leaves, leaf skeletons, or feathers

Glue stick

tools

Scissors or craft knife and cutting mat

Nature Cards

Color copies of natural materials can be used to make sophisticated and beautiful cards.

process

 On the sheet of heavy paper, draw an outline of your card that is ½ inch smaller all the way around than the actual card. If you can mark off more than one of these outlines on the same sheet of paper, do so. This will allow you to create more than one card from the same color-copied sheet.

❷ Select from your stockpile of found materials to create your design. Keep it simple and elegant. Arrange several items to your liking within the drawn boundaries, and adhere them with a glue stick.

❸ Place a clean piece of paper on top of the glued pieces, and rub the whole surface to make sure they're evenly adhered. Allow them to dry.

❹ Make color photocopies of the designs on a nice paper. (Again, copying a group of designs will save you money.)

❺ Carefully cut out the images with scissors or a craft knife. Glue them to the fronts of the cards and—voilà—you're done!

Stitched Lettering Cards

Use free-motion stitching to scribe letters on paper. Don't be daunted by
the stitching, since the charm of it lies in its imperfect, sketched look.

materials

Wallpaper swatches or other decorative papers of your choice

Sturdy paper such as construction paper or card stock

Spray adhesive

Mechanical pencil with soft eraser

Sewing thread

Decorative photo (optional)

Glue stick

tools

Metal ruler

Sewing machine with darning foot

Scissors

process

1 Decide on a size for your card (the square cards pictured here measure approximately 6 x 6 inches each). Keeping this size in mind, use spray adhesive to layer a sheet of decorative paper on top of sturdy paper.

2 If you want to place your text panel at the top of the card (as shown on the ciao card), cut out a shape from the layered paper that's the size of the card (when folded) plus about 2 inches at the top to serve as your text panel. This tab will be folded over later.

3 If you'd like to fill the front of the card with text (as shown on the *dear aunt Mary* card), cut a panel that's the size of the card when folded. Eventually, you'll attach this panel to the top of the back panel of the card.

4 For either card, decide on the placement of your text, and use the pencil and ruler to lightly mark guidelines on the decorative paper for the top and bottom lines. Draw the words lightly in pencil.

5 For free-motion stitching, drop the feed dogs on the sewing machine. Begin tracing the lettering with thread from the baseline at the left, through all the text, and ending at the right. As you stitch, you can thicken and embellish the letters. When you're done, erase the pencil lines and trim the tails of the thread.

6 If you're making the card with the tab at the top, you can now attach a decorative photo or more layered decorative paper to the tab to complete the front panel. Run a line of glue along the bottom edge of the tab on the front and adhere the piece.

7 Sew a decorative topstitch to secure the photo or paper to the tab. If you wish, open out the card and glue an additional piece of decorative paper inside the card for holding your message. Stitch around this piece.

8 To finish the full panel card, simply cut a back panel from sturdy paper, and sew the front panel to it along the top edge.

Layered, Torn, and Stitched Card

This striking card is made with the simplest of materials that have been assembled and randomly stitched together. Set your imagination free and have fun with this project!

materials

Card stock in several colors

Wallpaper swatches

Tissue paper

Glue stick

Postage stamps or other memorabilia

tools

Scissors or craft knife and
cutting mat

Sewing machine with capacity for
making a variety of stitches

Threads in various colors

process

1 Decide on the approximate size of your card and double the width. Cut out a piece of card stock about an inch larger than this dimension all the way around, leaving room for stitching.

2 Place a layer of wallpaper approximately the same size or smaller on top of the card stock. Tear the top edge or other edges as you wish.

3 Crumple up a piece of tissue paper. Glue it onto a piece of colored card stock to make a composite paper. Don't worry if it looks messy! Press it down beneath a book to flatten out the tissue paper. Let it dry.

4 Cut or tear the composite paper at the top in a design of your choice. Place it on top of the wallpaper, aligning it so that part of the paper shows behind it. Now you have three layers: the first, which serves as the card's inside, the second layer of wallpaper, and the third layer, which is a composite of tissue paper and card stock.

5 Fold the papers in half lengthwise to establish the card's middle. Fold the papers back out so that they're flat, and place the postage stamps on the front. Glue them in place and let them dry.

6 Once all the papers are *completely* dry, you're ready to sew. Place the paper with the design faceup under the machine's feed dogs and begin with the edges. Use zigzag and other fun stitch variations in different colors to complete your design. Frame the stamps with stitching if you wish.

7 There's no right or wrong way to stitch your card, but to make sure that all the layers are secured, it's a good idea to sew some lines of basic stitching around the edges and up the middle. From there, you can use different stitches, both curved and straight, to create a design on top of and through the layers.

Elegant Stitched Cards

Use handmade papers and waxed linen to create these artistic cards. The lines of
hand stitching complement the arrangement of small paper shapes.

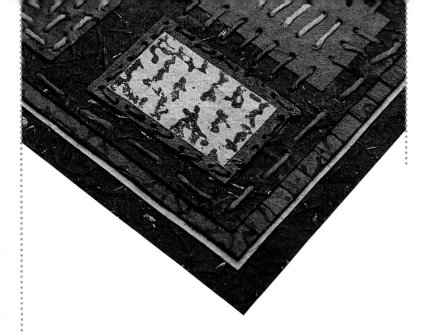

materials

Heavy card stock or handmade paper for card and envelope

Text-weight paper

Construction paper

Assorted handmade paper swatches or other nice papers

White craft glue

Piece of insulation board or layered cardboard, at least 8 inches square

Waxed linen in various colors

Envelope template (see page 142)

Double-sided tape, ½ inch wide

tools

Scissors

Craft knife and cutting mat

Metal ruler

Bone folder

Small awl or needle tool

Size 18 sewing needle

Heavy book

process

1 Cut a piece of heavy paper into a 5 x 10-inch rectangle. Fold it in half to form a 5-inch square card. Crease the folded edge with a bone folder. Set it aside.

2 Cut a 4¾ x 9¾ rectangle from the text-weight paper. Fold it to form a square and crease it with the bone folder. Set it aside.

3 Choose a background paper for the front of the card. You'll layer cutout design elements on top of this piece and stitch them before eventually attaching the piece to the front of the card. If you wish, you can layer more than one square piece to create more depth.

4 Cut the main background piece to a size slightly smaller than the card's dimensions. If you're adding more pieces on top, cut these out and glue them in place.

5 To create your design, experiment with various shapes cut from construction paper in different arrangements. Once you're satisfied with your design, use these templates to cut out the final pieces. Glue them to the background piece, and press it underneath a heavy book until dry.

6 Place the piece faceup on insulation board or several layers of cardboard. Use a thin awl to punch the stitching holes. Use the ruler to guide you if you're making straight lines or want to keep the stitches the same size and distance apart.

7 After punching the holes, thread your needle and bring it up through one of the holes, leaving a tail of a few inches on the back of the piece. There's no need to worry about securing the tail, because it will be glued down later on. Proceed with your stitching, using different threads.

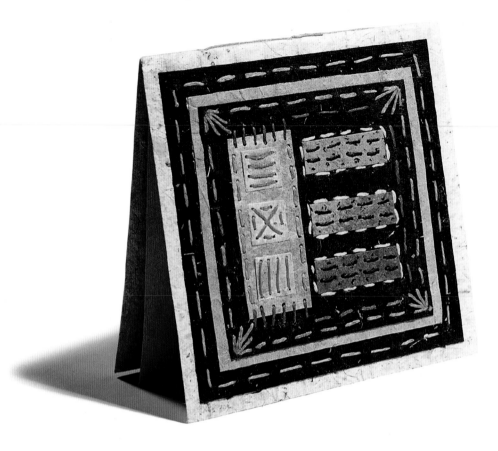

8 After you've finished the stitching, glue the decorated piece to the front of the card. Press it until it is dry.

9 Place the liner paper inside the card and center it. Along the fold inside, measure in 2½ inches to the center and pierce a hole with the awl. Pierce two more holes along the fold located an inch from each end. Use a pamphlet stitch to secure the liner to the card.

10 Use the template to cut out the envelope from a heavy paper that complements the card. Score and crease the fold lines with the bone folder.

11 If you want to add a stitched mailing label, cut out a piece of paper and stitch it to the front of the envelope following the same steps you used to stitch the card.

12 When you're ready to seal the envelope, place the card inside it. Fold in the two side flaps followed by the bottom flap, securing them with double-sided tape. Add a strip of tape to the top flap and leave the protective paper side intact until you're ready to remove it and seal the envelope.

Circular Stitched Cards and Tags

These whimsical cards and tags give you a chance to express
your creativity! Layer decorative and found papers on heavier paper,
and then cut out circles in different sizes before assembling them.

materials

Wallpaper, sewing patterns, tissue paper, postage stamps, or other interesting decorative papers

Sturdy paper such as construction paper or card stock

Spray adhesive

Sewing threads for machine

Large buttons

Heavy thread for sewing buttons

Ribbon

tools

Sewing machine

Circular compass with pencil

Scissors

Hole punch

Sewing needle

process

1 Layer decorative paper(s) over sturdy paper and adhere it with spray adhesive. If you're using sewing patterns or tissue paper, try wadding them up and unfolding them so they're textured before applying them.

2 Randomly machine-stitch across the papers, using various decorative stitches and colors of thread. Cut loose and have fun!

3 Use the compass to draw circles of various circumferences ranging from about 2 to 6 inches and cut them out. Erase any pencil marks.

4 To make the layered button cards, stack several circles of various diameters one on top of the other, moving from larger to smaller (or simply use two large circles). Cut one of the circles from unstitched paper so you'll have a surface on which to write your message. If you're using several stacked circles, add this unstitched circle to your pile near the middle of the stack.

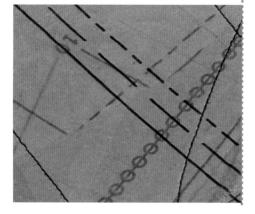

5 When you're satisfied with the arrangement, use the hole punch to punch a hole at the top of all of the circles except for the largest, bottom one. Place a large button on top of the stacked holes. Thread the needle with heavy thread and pull it through the back of the bottom circular layer.

6 Push the needle through the punched holes in the stacked circles, being careful not to punch/sew the paper, or you won't be able to pivot the circles. Sew back down through the other buttonhole and through the punched holes to the back of the card. Run the thread through the holes a few times to make the button secure. When you're done, tie the thread off at the back and cover the threads with a small piece of adhered paper.

7 To make a chain of circles to use as a card or an unusual tag, punch two holes on either side of each paper circle. Weave ribbon through each circle, moving down through the first hole and back up through the one on the other side before moving on to connect the next circle.

8 When you're finished, use a decorative stitch to sew down the ribbon on each circle on both sides. Trim all the threads.

9 To create single circular tags, simply thread a stitched circle with ribbon, and create a loop at the top to hold the two ends of the ribbon in place.

Altered Cards and Tags

Cover slide mounts with torn book pages to create small frames for enclosing stamped images. Add other ephemera and fibers to create a particular mood.

materials

Cards and tags in colors of your choice

Envelopes

Slide mounts (available at a photography store)

Old book pages or maps

White craft glue

Inkpads in shades that complement papers

Patterned, word, and facial rubber stamps

Double-sided tape

Antique papers that compliment cards, such as tea-dyed papers

Embellishments such as scrapbooking images or stamped and cutout images

Colorful fibers or ribbons for tags

tools

Craft knife and cutting mat

Metal ruler

process

1 Cut a square piece of paper from your book page or map that measures an inch larger than your slide mount all the way around. For instance, if you're using a standard 2 x 2-inch mount, cut a piece of paper that measures 4 x 4 inches.

2 Glue the slide mount to the center of the paper on the back side.

3 Use a craft knife to trim the paper next to each corner on a diagonal, leaving a margin of about ¼ inch for folding the paper on the mount at each corner. Fold the paper at each corner and glue it in place (figure 1).

4 Next, trim the paper in lines parallel to each side, leaving ¼ inch to overlap on the mount. Fold the paper on the mount again and glue it in place, creating a smooth edge (figure 2).

5 To cover the central edges of the mount, cut the paper inside from one corner to the other, making an X-configuration. Then cut out a rectangular shape that leaves a ¼-inch margin that you can fold onto the mount (figure 3). As you did on the outside edges, fold the papers and adhere them, smoothing them to create a nice edge.

6 After you've covered the mounts that you wish to use and they are dry, rub them with ink from the inkpads. Layer the inks to create a mottled effect.

7 Stamp faces on tea-dyed paper or other antique-looking paper, and cut them to fit behind the mounts. Attach them with glue.

8 Create backgrounds on the cards and tags with stamped images or layered papers. Stamped and torn papers create a nice look. Adhere any papers that you're using for your background.

9 Use double-sided tape to attach a framed piece to each card or tag.

10 As accents, add embellishments to your cards and tags (such as scrapbooking or stamped and cut paper images). Add fibers or ribbons to the tags for fringe.

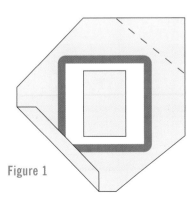

Figure 1

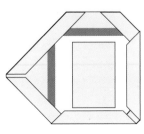

Figure 2

Figure 3

Suite of "Found" Angel Cards

These imaginative cards and tags allow you to turn your ancestors,
whether real or adopted, into heavenly beings!

materials

Cards and envelopes in black
or white

Tags

Cards and tags in various sizes of
your choice

Colored photocopies of vintage
photos

Paper and foil wings (available
at scrapbooking stores or craft
supply stores) or color photocopies
of wings

Pages from an old book

Gold ribbon and twine

Clear dots (available in craft
supply stores)

tools

Scissors

Clear-drying craft glue or glue stick

process

1 When you color-copy your photos, enlarge or reduce the figures or wings as needed to fit your cards. Use scissors to carefully cut out the shapes.

2 Position the components on cards and tags, trying out different combinations of wings and figures. Keep proportions in mind when you do this.

3 Place the wings behind the figures.

4 Tear swatches of paper from old book pages to place behind the winged figures. Glue down all the layers, and let them dry.

5 Adhere embellishments such as ribbon, twine, or dots to your design.

6 Add gold cord to the tags, and fray the edges if you wish.

Forgotten Dreams Cards

This suite of tags and cards makes one think of watery depths
and dreamlike states. A stream-of-consciousness approach to collage
and mixed media can lead to all kinds of discoveries.

materials

Old book pages

Regular-sized cards and mini-tags

Playing cards

Green acrylic paint

Acrylic gel medium

Cards in off-white (antique) or black

Rubber stamps with designs such as
ferns, facial images, Gothic-style
lettering

Permanent inkpads in dark shades
of green or blue

Textured threads and fibers

Small seashells or other found
objects

tools

Scissors

Flat artist's paintbrush
(size 12 or 16)

Damp cloth

process

1 Cut or tear old book pages to use as background papers for your cards or tags. Select some playing cards to use as well.

2 Brush the acrylic paint over the pages and cards and let it dry slightly. Gently swipe the surfaces with a damp cloth. You'll pick up the still-wet paint while leaving the dry paint behind. The surface will pick up the texture of the cloth. Parts of the book text or printed card will show beneath the wash. Allow the papers to dry.

3 Cut the background book papers to a size of your choice for layering on your card. Use gel medium to adhere the papers and the cards.

4 Stamp images on top of these washed surfaces with darker ink. If you wish, add stamped lettering to form words. You can also add small painted and stamped tags for embellishment.

5 As a final step, add textured threads to the tags and glue on found objects such as small seashells.

Black & White Serendipity Cards

This unique project allows you to cut loose and stamp random designs before framing selected parts with a stamped line. The monochromatic palette makes them all the more striking.

materials

White and black cardstock

Rubber stamp that prints a square frame or square eraser for carving

Various word and themed rubber stamps of your choice

Inkpads in shades of grey as well as black and white

White craft glue or glue stick

Cards and tags in white, gray, or black

Black and white decorative ribbons for fringe

White and black envelopes

tools

Carving tool, such as a linoleum carver (optional)

Scissors or craft knife, cutting mat, and metal ruler

Heavy book

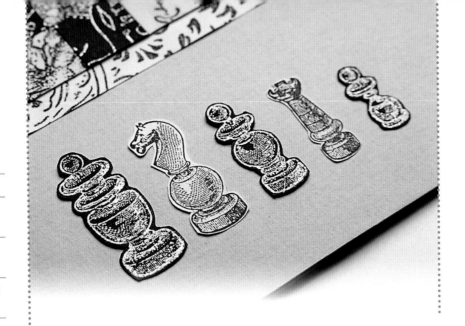

process

1　The squares on these cards and tags are formed with a simple line that serves as a frame. You can create this effect with a premade rubber stamp that prints a square, or you can carve your own from an eraser. If you carve your own, you'll have more control over the look of the line.

2　On the blank white cardstock or other nice paper print randomly in black ink with various stamps. Follow up with layers of gray and white stamping. On the black paper, print randomly with white and gray ink.

3　Make sure the sheets are covered with overlapping stamping. Use the square stamp or carved eraser to print borders around areas of your choice. Come up with a mixture of black and white papers so that you can alternate the squares on your cards.

4 Cut out the squares with scissors or a craft knife. Place these squares in a pattern of your choice on either black or white cardstock that is trimmed to fit the front of your cards and leave a margin around the edges. You can also add an extra layer of white or black card stock underneath a designed panel, if you wish. Adhere the squares to the panel and allow it to dry slightly before adhering the panel to the card. Press under a heavy book to dry. Use this same process to create patterned tags.

5 You can leave the card as it is or add a foreground image (such as the woman shown on the left-hand card in the photo). Stamp the image of your choice on cardstock, and cut it out before adhering it to the card. Now the checkerboard motif serves as the background for your image. Add lines to the image with a black felt-tip pen if you wish.

6 If you wish, embellish the cards with black and white fringe on the spines and add it to the tops of the tags. As a final touch, stamp your envelopes with a complimentary design motif.

Variation: Instead of framing up squares from your randomly stamped designs, cut the papers into strips and weave them to form a checkerboard design of contrasting blacks and whites. It's easy—simply alternate a black strip and a white strip in both directions.

Monogram Wedding Invitations

For a wedding or other important life event, there is still nothing that equals the impact of hand-lettered cards. The following instructions give you steps for lettering the two cards shown here. If your event involves lots of people, you can take your original lettered art to a printer and have invitations printed. Or you can scan the artwork and print out duplicates on a high-quality printer.

materials

Black ink

Ruled tracing paper

2H Pencil

Masking tape

tools

T-square

Drafting table or slanted board

Broad-edged calligraphy pen and nibs (larger for monogram and smaller for envelope lettering)

Light box

Paintbrush for mixing paint

Tray for mixing paint

Kneaded eraser

Earth Tone
Italic Monogram

This monogram is done in Italic uppercase lettering. You can use the same technique to scribe other styles of lettering.

materials

Pre-cut blank watercolor greeting card and matching envelope

Olive, raw umber, and white gouache paint

process

1 Use ruled tracing paper, black ink, and a broad-edged pen to experiment with different lettering designs in a size that fits your card. Interweave the letters while retaining the essence of their classic forms.

2 When you're pleased with the design, tape it to the light box and position the card on top, making sure it's centered and square with the card's edges. Trace the monogram and any guidelines onto the card stock with the pencil.

3 Squeeze out a small dab of raw umber and white gouache into a tray. With a paintbrush dipped in water, add a few drops of water at a time until the paint has the consistency of light cream. On a piece of scrap paper, test the paint in the pen to make sure it's thin enough to flow but thick enough to create the desired color. Mix the olive green with a dab of white in another tray and test it for consistency. Let the test sample dry to make sure the color is correct.

4 Dip the nib of the pen into the raw umber mixture and draw the first letter of the monogram. Rinse the nib and reservoir thoroughly, and dip the pen into the olive green mixture and draw the second letter. Let the monogram dry completely before gently and carefully erasing the pencil lines.

5 To scribe the address on a coordinating envelope, rule the envelope with light pencil lines and write it with a smaller pen nib. Let the ink dry completely before gently and carefully erasing the pencil lines.

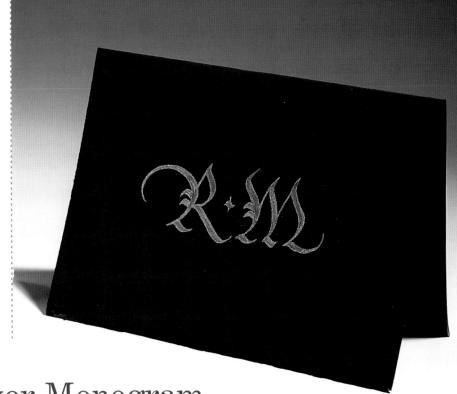

Silver Monogram on Black Paper

This monogram is done in Gothic uppercase lettering. Again, you can apply the described technique to any lettering you choose.

materials

Pre-cut black cards made of smooth, heavy paper with matching envelope

Erasable transfer paper in a light color

Silver ink

Triple-zero paintbrush

process

1 Using ruled tracing paper, black ink, and the wide pen nib, experiment with arrangements of the letters of your choice until you like the effect. Pencil in the perimeters of the card on the tracing paper, making sure to center and align the monogram.

2 Open out and tape the black card to the drafting table or slanted board. Place the monogram design over the card and tape it at the top, making sure to position the design so that the penciled in edge of the card matches the edge of the black card. Slip a piece of transfer paper between the design and card and gently trace the monogram. Remove the transfer paper and lift up the tracing paper to make sure the whole design has been transferred.

3 Use silver ink and a clean wide pen nib to draw the monogram onto the black paper. Touch ups can be done with the triple-zero brush and silver ink. Carefully erase any traces of the erasable transfer paper with a kneaded eraser.

4 Scribe the address of the recipient on a matching envelope as described for the previous monogram.

Stylish Portfolio Card

This handsome card made with faux leather paper will turn the head of even the
most discriminating person. The insert for writing a personal note slides out so that
the recipient can keep this nice piece on his or her desk to hold notes or photos.

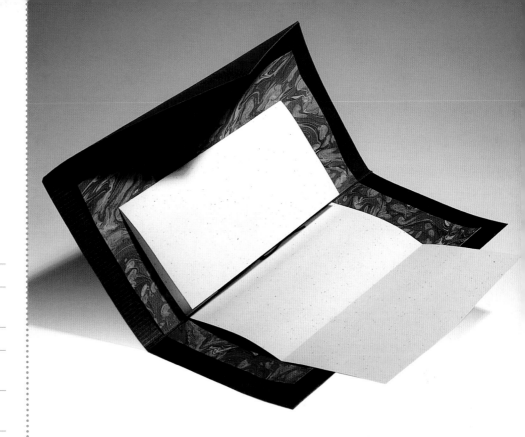

materials

Templates (see page 138)

Black ribbed card stock (inside cover)

Spray adhesive

Decorative paper with faux leather finish (cover)

Marbled paper or other decorative paper (inside, background)

Thin ribbon or cord and tassel

Smooth natural paper (insert)

Small dot of black hook-and-loop tape

tools

Craft knife and cutting mat

Metal ruler

Bone folder

process

1 Use the cover template as a guide to cut out the inside cover from the black ribbed card stock. Use spray adhesive to attach it to the faux leather finish paper.

2 Place the piece on your cutting mat with the black paper facing you and cut around the edge to trim the other paper.

3 Use the bone folder to score and fold the cover where indicated on the template.

4 Cut out the decorative background paper by following the template and fold it in half where indicated. Spray the back of it with spray adhesive and position it inside of the cover along the fold line.

5 Tie the thin cord around the fold, placing the tassel on the outside spine of the cover.

6 Cut the insert according to the template and fold it as indicated. Slide the insert underneath the cord to hold it in place.

7 Close the card and position the hook-and-loop dot underneath the pointed tip to serve as a closure.

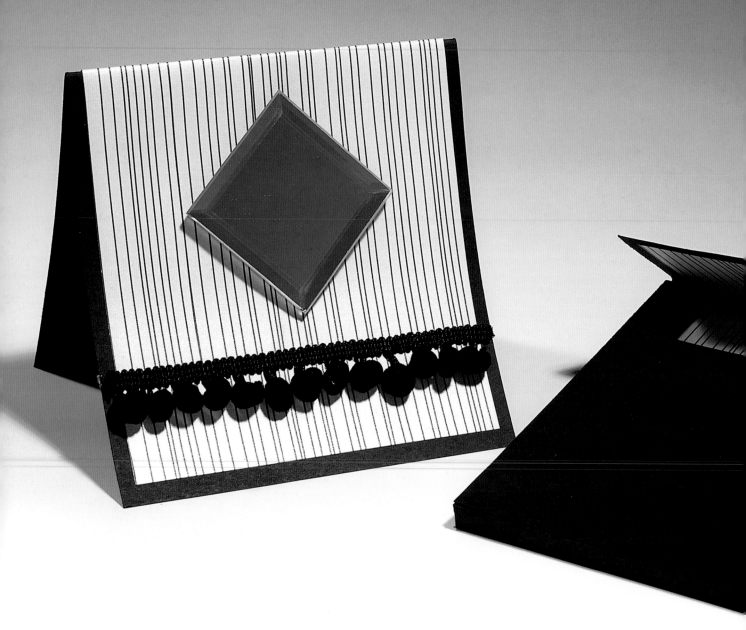

Mirrored Cards

Retro-look striped papers and mirrors make a classy combination.
Add a touch of pom-pom trim or ribbon to sass it up!

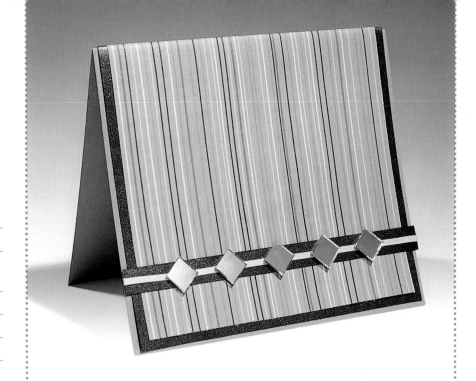

materials

Card stock in color of your choice

Striped decorative papers
  or wallpaper

White craft glue or glue stick

Pom-pom trim

Small mirror or mirrors

Strong adhesive

Narrow ribbon (option)

Envelope template (page 139)

tools

Scissors or craft knife and
  cutting mat

Bone folder

process

1 From the card stock, cut a square-shaped card in a size of your choice, placing the fold at the top. Use a bone folder to score and fold the card in half.

2 Cut a piece of striped paper that is about ¼ inch smaller than the card's dimensions. Adhere the piece to the card, leaving a border around it.

3 Cut a piece of pom-pom trim to fit across the bottom of the card, and glue it in place. Use strong adhesive to attach the mirror to the card so that it sits diagonally, above the trim.

4 Use the same card stock as the card to make the envelope. Line it with a piece of the striped paper, if you wish.

Variation: Decorate the bottom of the card with a row of tiny mirrors placed diagonally on top of a metallic-finish paper strip topped with a narrow cloth ribbon.

Small Book-Cards

This handsome little book-card conceals sticky-note pads. Write a greeting
to a friend on the first sheet, and she can use the rest of the sticky notes
until they're gone—and then restock your card with new ones!

materials

Self-stick notepad in size of your choice

Mat board or book board

Handmade, designer, or paste papers for outside cover

Diluted white glue (3 parts glue to 1 part water)

Wax paper

Lightweight decorative or colored paper for inside cover

Tacky glue

For cover decoration: scraps of nice papers along with embellishments such as polymer clay cane (available in craft supply stores), small coins, scrapbooking trinkets, copper tape, wire, or natural materials

Strong adhesive for embellishments

Raffia (optional)

tools

Mat knife

Craft knife and cutting mat

T-square

Glue brush

Heavy book

Scissors

process

1 The common size of a self-stick notepad is 3 x 3 inches, and the directions that follow are based on that dimension. Regardless, always add ⅛ inch to the size of the pad all the way around to determine the dimension for both your front and back cover. The spine should always be cut to the height of the pad with the width determined by the pad's thickness plus double that of the book board.

2 Based on a 3 x 3-inch pad, use the mat knife to cut three pieces of book board: two 3¼ x 3¼-inch pieces for the front and back covers and a 3¼-inch-high spine that's approximately the thickness of the pad plus twice the thickness of the book board.

3 Place the pieces side-by side with the spine in the middle, leaving about 1/16 inch between it and the two covers. Take the overall measurement of this composite piece, both length and width, and add about ½ inch all the way around to that measurement. Cut your cover paper to this size (in this case, 8 x 4¼ inches).

4 Coat one side of the cover pieces with diluted white glue and position them as before on the paper, leaving the margin around the edges.

5 Lay a sheet of wax paper on top of the cover and press it overnight underneath heavy books. (If you're pressing several covers at once, be sure to place wax paper between each.)

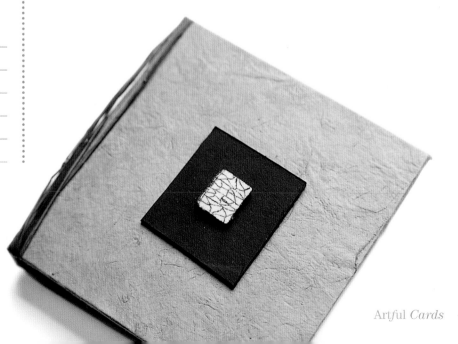

6 Trim the decorative paper around the cover pieces, leaving a border of about ½ inch for folding inside.

7 Turn in each of the four corners of the cover paper to the inside at a 45° angle. Adhere them with tacky glue. Allow the paper to dry a bit before turning in the sides, top, and bottom edges. Adhere these with tacky glue.

8 Cut the inside cover paper so that it's ¼ to ⅛ inch smaller than the cover all the way around. Coat this paper with diluted white glue and adhere it, covering part of the cover paper that's already been turned inside. Place it beneath a heavy book and let it dry.

9 Use tacky glue to adhere the self-stick notepad to the inside cover. Decorate the front of the book-card in any way that you like. Layer it with a swatch of nice paper and a slice of polymer clay cane, as shown here, or come up with any number of other possibilities such as decorating it with embossed stamping, metallic leaf or copper tape, or natural materials. Use strong glue to attach any embellishments.

10 Keep your cover design simple and elegant rather than cluttering it up, in tune with the elegant cover papers.

11 If you wish, wrap some raffia around the spine of the cover and tie it off, or use it to tie up the whole booklet like a gift.

Black Cat Card

BOO! This hair-raising black cat, with
its glittery coat, is sure to delight any
kid on this delightfully scary day.

materials

Templates for cat and bat
(page 139)

Orange cards and matching
envelopes

Sheet of black construction paper

Sheet of yellow construction paper

Glitter glue

Yellow mulberry paper

Alphabet stamps and black inkpad

tools

Small scissors

Craft knife

process

1 Cut out the templates and trace the shapes onto black construction paper. Use small scissors to carefully cut them out from the paper.

2 Use the craft knife to cut the delicate holes that form the cat's eyes. Cut out a small piece of yellow construction paper that fits behind them. Wipe the yellow paper with glitter glue, and position the paper on the back of the cat's head so that the sparkle shows through. Allow the papers to dry.

3 Wipe glitter glue on the cat and the bat to lend them sheen. Allow the glue to dry.

4 Cut out a banner from yellow mulberry paper. Glue it in place and let it dry.

5 Position the cat and bat, and glue them in place. (Notice the nice effect created by allowing the cat's tail to overlap the banner.)

6 After the glue dries, use alphabet stamps to spell out "Halloween" or a greeting of your choice on the banner. (Don't worry if your stamped lettering flows over onto the card; it adds to the handmade, artistic look of it.)

Fall Mail-Art Card

What better way is there to embrace the change from summer to autumn
than by making and sending this beautiful mail-art card to a friend? Stashed among
the bills and junk mail, it will be a welcome surprise for anyone.

materials

Mat board in two contrasting earthtones

4 brass paper brads

White craft glue

Decorative paper

Sticky label paper

Patterned stamps that resemble fabric

Inkpads in appropriate colors

Autumn-themed stamps such as leaves, squirrels, pumpkins, or jack-o'-lanterns

Markers or colored pencils

Sticky label tape

tools

Mat knife

Cutting mat

Metal ruler or straightedge

Hammer and nail

Decorative-edged scissors that cut a ragged edge

Decorative-edged scissors that cut a "postage stamp" edge

process

1 On your cutting mat, cut one piece of mat board into a large rectangle and then cut another smaller rectangle that fits on top of it, leaving a nice margin around the edges.

2 Place the smaller piece of mat board on a pile of newspapers or an old magazine. Decide where you want to place the brads and mark the points with a pencil. Use the hammer and the nail to punch holes through the two boards at these points. Placed the smaller rectangular piece in position on top of the larger one, and use it as a guide to create four holes. Attach the brads through the holes.

3 Apply a thin layer of glue to the back of the piece and place it on top of the decorative paper. Smooth out any wrinkles and let them dry.

4 Use a mat knife to carefully trim around the rectangle. Now your card is ready for decorating!

5 Use fabric-patterned stamps and different colors of ink to decorate the sticky label paper. Cut out the pieces with ragged edge scissors. Stamp the decorative paper with autumn stamps, cut out the pieces, and adhere them to the stamped sticky label paper. Use a marker to draw decorative borders around them to create the look of a frame. Use colored markers or pens to fill in the frame's color.

6 Apply these decorative elements to both the front and the back of the piece, leaving room for a mailing label. If you wish, draw theme pictures, such as pumpkins, leaves, or nuts on pieces of paper, and cut them out with the scissors so they resemble postage stamps. Adhere these to the back of the piece.

7 Write autumn themed-words on sticky label tape and cut them out with "postage stamp" decorative-edged scissors. Apply them as your final touch to the sticky paper designs.

8 Create a simple mailing label from decorative paper.

Fabric Pumpkin Card

Inspired by a pumpkin festival held each year in this designer's hometown,
this fanciful fabric card is perfect for children. Who doesn't love a bright orange pumpkin?

materials

Assortment of fabrics (striped, patterned, light and dark orange, yellow, black, and green)

Orange and black thread

Alphabet rubber stamps

Black inkpad

Two decorative buttons

One snap set

tools

Scissors

Sewing machine

Fabric glue

Sewing needle

process

1 Cut out two sets of house shapes from both patterned fabric and light orange fabric. Sew one set of patterned and orange together with a random, curved stitching (such as a darning freestyle quilting stitch). Leave the fabric edges torn and frayed. This is the central portion of the card.

2 Sew together the other set of patterned and orange house pieces, using another random, curved stitch. After it's sewn together, cut the house piece in half to form two doors.

3 Create the borders by ripping striped fabric into strips. Cut a length to fit along each side of the house and doors. Adhere the strips with fabric glue, and allow them to dry. When dry, stitch them in place with a couple of lines of orange thread.

4 Cut a pumpkin shape out of the darker orange fabric. Glue it in place inside the house. Cut and glue on fabric eyes and a mouth of light orange as well as a green stem. After the glue dries, use black thread to stitch the edges of the pumpkin in place. Sew more lines of black stitching to define the grooves. Stitch around the eyes and stitch lines to make a scary pumpkin grin. Stitch the stem with a random stitch to add texture.

5 Cut three strips of yellow fabric to fit the doors and inside panel. Stamp your greeting on these strips. Sew them in place.

6 Create a latch by randomly stitching two pieces of black fabric together with orange thread. By hand, sew the left edge to the outside of the left door with a small, inconspicuous stitch. Then sew a button on top of the stitch.

7 Place the doors on top of the house, and stitch the edges together so the doors open to reveal the pumpkin inside. (Don't sew along the rooflines.)

8 Close the doors and mark where the latch falls on the right door. By hand, sew on a snap set, one side to the latch and the matching side to the door. Sew the other decorative button on top.

Pop-Up Barnyard Card

This adorable card is sure to delight any child when he opens it and discovers
pop-up animals and an old-fashioned red barn.

materials

5 x 7-inch blank card and
  envelope

Decorative paper with farm theme

Card stock in light blue, light
  green, yellow, and beige

Heavy red paper

Glue stick or rubber cement

Instant-bonding glue

Farm animal stickers

tools

Craft knife and cutting mat

Bone folder

Decorative-edged scissors

Metal ruler

process

Cut a 10 x 7-inch piece from the decorative background paper. Open out the card. Glue the decorative paper to the front/outside of the card.

Cut a 5 x 7-inch rectangle from both green and blue card stock. Glue the papers inside the blank card, one color to each panel. The blue panel will become the sky, and the green will be the ground.

To create the barn, cut a 4½ x 10-inch piece from the heavy red paper and create a series of widthwise folds in it. Make the first fold 3½ inches from the short edge. Then progress on to make an accordion fold with a series of six folds that are ½ inch apart. After that's done, fold the paper under, 2 inches away from the final fold.

Cut a 1½ x 4-inch piece from beige card stock, and adhere it to the back of the red piece at the bottom where it fits between the edge and the final fold. Cut a 3½ x 4-inch piece from beige card stock, and attach it to the large space on the back so that it meets the other edge. These pieces serve as reinforcement for the pop-up barn.

Place the red piece flat on your cutting mat with the largest fold at the top and the smaller, 1½-inch fold at the bottom. Find the center of the first fold and mark it lightly with a pencil. Center and cut a 1½-inch slit along the fold. Cut a second one parallel to it and 1 inch above it. Then cut a perpendicular slit right down the middle between the two horizontal cuts. Fold the paper out to form doors.

6 Open up your card and position the barn inside it with the doors at the bottom of the green side. Fold the reinforced flap underneath and back it up to the fold so that the doors are positioned on the ground plane. Glue this piece in place.

7 To attach the top of the barn, glue the outside (red side) of the larger reinforced section to the blue background. The two reinforced tabs should now meet at the fold in the card. The roof of the barn will pop up in the middle.

8 From a corner of a piece of yellow card stock, use decorative scissors to cut out a rounded piece with a 1½-inch radius. Adhere the "sun" to the upper right corner of your card.

9 Next you'll add the pop-up cows. Begin by cutting a strip of green card stock that measures ½ x 5½ inches

to serve as an attachment for one of the cows. Make three widthwise folds in the card stock: 1 inch from one end and ½ and 1½ inches from the other end. Position the 1-inch tab between the barn and the right edge of the card so that the ½-inch-wide edge of it sits on the fold. (The rest of the strip will extend out from this attached piece.) Adhere this tab with the instant-bond glue.

10 Fold under the tab on the other end of the strip. Put a dab of glue on the outer face of it (the one that will touch the card), and fold the card together so that it sticks to the green ground. Allow it to dry.

11 Glue two cow stickers to a piece of the green card stock for reinforcement, and cut out the shapes with the craft knife. Open the card and use instant bonding glue to attach one cow to the front of the strip.

12 To make the other cow-holding tab, cut a ½ x 4-inch strip from the green card stock. Fold it from one end at 1 inch, then 2½ inches, and finally 3 inches.

13 Glue the first 1-inch tab to the barn beside the door. Repeat the previous step of folding in the final outermost tab and gluing it in place with the card shut. Allow it to dry before attaching the second cow.

14 If you wish, add some animal stickers inside the barn so that they show through the open doors. Add other stickers of your choice to the scenery.

Moving Right Along Card

Create a memorable change-of-address card that won't get tossed in the trash! Duplicate this card on a color photocopier to send out to all of your friends.

materials

White cards and matching envelopes

Blue acrylic paint

Acrylic matte medium, white craft glue, or a glue stick

Colored pencil or pen

Butterfly-wing scrapbooking stickers

Colored paper for insert

tools

Artist's paintbrush

Color photocopier

Scissors

Heavy book

Craft knife and cutting mat

Metal ruler

process

1 Open out the card and lay it flat. Use loose brushstrokes to paint a blue sky on the front of the card, leaving some white edges.

2 Tear a small piece of the map to fit along the bottom of your card to create the effect of land and a horizon. Glue it in place on the card.

3 On the front of the card, use a colored pencil to sketch a house shape. Make the shape tilted, as if it's about to take flight.

4 Use a color copier to duplicate as many copies of the front of the card as you need. Trim each to fit the front of the remaining cards, and glue them into place with a glue stick. Insert blank pieces of paper between them, and place them underneath a heavy object or pile of books to dry flat.

5 Place each card flat on your cutting mat and use the craft knife to cut out each window. After you're done, paste butterfly wings on either side of the house.

6 On a colored paper insert, print our your new address, leaving room for a handwritten message above it. Cut the insert to fit inside the card, and hand write "We've moved!" so that it shows through the cut window.

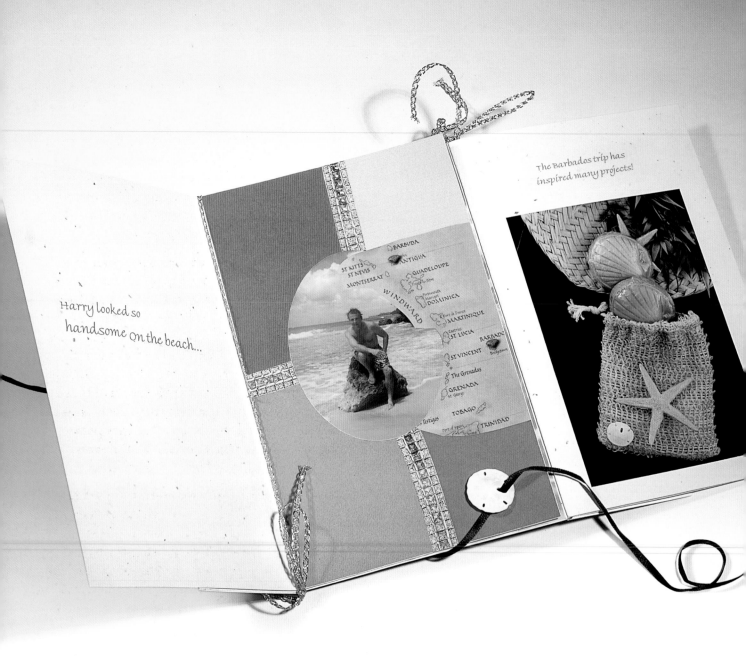

Harry looked so
handsome on the beach...

The Barbados trip has
inspired many projects!

Storybook Greeting Card

This many-paged card gives you plenty of room to describe
your latest trip or other important event. Easy to assemble,
this book/card can convey your best memories.

materials

3 sheets of card stock, each
  8½ x 11 inches

Thick decorative paper

Photo adhesive

Photographs and other paper
  memorabilia

Transparent address labels or sheets
  of colorful paper (for text)

Matching thin ribbon

Found objects or trinkets (optional)

tools

Metal ruler

Bone folder

Craft knife and cutting mat

Scissors

Heavy book

Computer or label-making program
  (for text)

process

1 On a piece of the card stock, score two fold lines located 2¾ inches in from each of the 8½-inch-wide ends of the paper. Fold the panels in so they meet in the center. This folded piece will serve as your cover.

2 Trim off ¼ inch from the 8½-inch end of each of the remaining two card stock pieces and fold each sheet in half. Set these pieces aside.

3 To decorate the outside of the cover, cut two pieces of thick decorative paper that measure 2¾ x 8½ inches each. Glue them in place on front of the wings. Cut a 5½ x 8½-inch panel of decorative paper for the back of the cover, and glue it in place between the decorated wings. Press the cover underneath a book for an hour.

4 Before you begin to compose the narrative for the storybook, you need to understand the order of the pages. When you open out the card, the story begins on the panel inside the left wing. The narrative continues on the front of one of the pieces of folded card stock (which will be attached to the cover later at the fold) and runs through the remaining three pages. Then the narrative picks up on the front of the second piece of folded card stock (which will also be attached to the cover along the other fold) and run through those pages. The story will conclude on the back inside panel.

5 Use photographs, mementos, and decorative paper to weave a story inside your card, pasting them throughout the book. Keep in mind that the first image(s) and word(s) are like your greeting to the recipient, such as— "we had…fun in Barbados!" Try to recreate the feel of the trip or other event through appropriate color; interesting facts or thoughts, and vivid imagery. It's nice to create a different feeling on each page.

6 Create text to use with a label-making program and transparent labels, or print out text on your computer on colorful printer paper. After you've composed your story, press parts underneath a heavy book for a while.

7 Use ribbon to attach each of the folded pieces to the inside folds of the cover. Tie the bottom inside card to the right side and then the top inside card to the left side. Tie the card closed with the same ribbon. Embellish the outside of the card with found objects or trinkets.

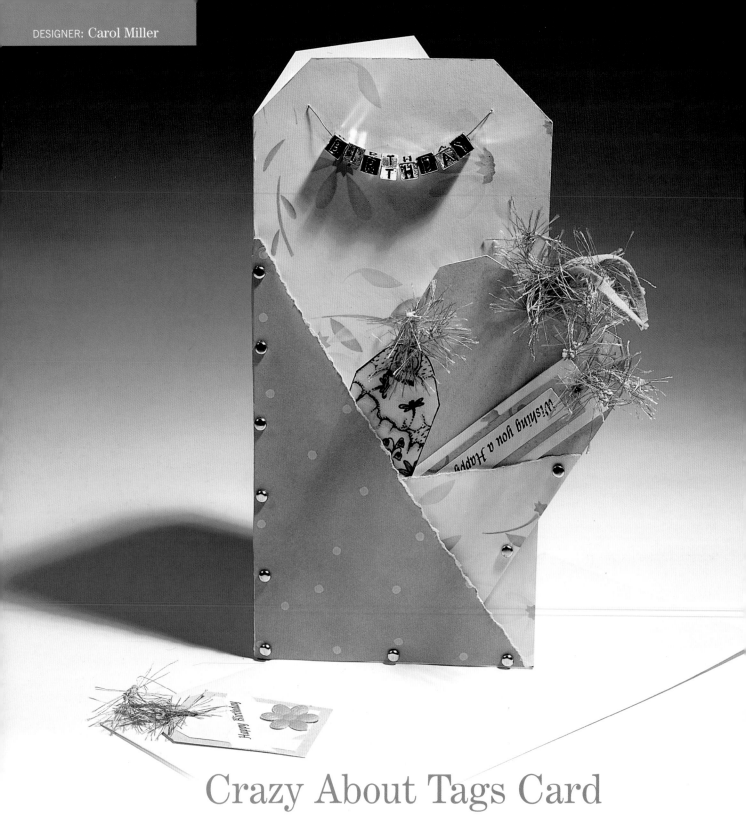

Crazy About Tags Card

The current tag craze led to this idea of creating a large tag-shaped card for nesting tags within tags. Discovering the one that's tucked inside with a scribed message is a treat for the recipient.

materials

White card stock

Decorative scrapbooking papers in coordinating colors

Colored brads

Garden-theme rubber stamp

Permanent black inkpad

Fine-tipped black pen

Colored pencils

Acrylic gloss medium

Coordinating ribbon and eyelash fibers

Thin silver wire

Metal alphabet beads (available at craft supply stores)

Text-weight paper

tools

Scissors or craft knife and cutting mat

Metal ruler

Bone folder

White craft glue or glue stick

Hole punch

Computer

Small paintbrush

Embroidery needle

Clear cellophane tape

Double-sided tape

process

1 Cut an 8 x 8-inch square (or size of your choice) from the white card stock. Fold it in half and smooth the edge with a bone folder. Trim off top corners of the card to make it resemble a tag.

2 Trace the card shape onto a piece of decorative paper. Cut out the paper and glue it to the front of your card.

3 To form the pocket, begin by ripping a sheet of the decorative paper in half. Position the torn edge on the front of your card from close to the top of the left edge down to the bottom right corner. Trim the paper to fit along the edge of the card.

4 Make marks where you want to place the brads on the decorative paper and the front of the card along the edge of it. Attach the brads to hold the pocket in place.

5 Cut a 3 x 5-inch tag from the white card stock, trimming the corners as you did the larger card. Cut and glue another sheet of coordinating paper on it. Allow it to dry, and then form a pocket on the tag by attaching a torn piece of decorative paper across the tag, this time from the top right side down to the left corner. Again, attach brads to hold the pocket in place.

6 Stamp the garden image on white card stock. Draw the shape of a small tag on top of the printed image with the black pen. Within these boundaries, color in the images with colored pencils.

7 Cut out your stamped image tag and punch a hole at the top. Coat the tag with the acrylic gloss medium. After it dries, thread and tie some decorative eyelash fringe or ribbon through the top of the tag.

11 String alphabet beads and the word "birthday" or another message on a length of silver wire. Thread the ends of the wire through the holes and allow the lettering to drape down like a necklace. Once it is placed, trim off the excess wire on the back and tape down the ends.

12 On text-weight paper, print out a message for inside your card. Fold and cut the piece to fit inside the card and tack it in place on the inside left with double-sided tape, covering up the bits of taped wire and the backs of the brads. Leave the other side of the insert unattached for a nice effect.

8 From your computer, print out a fun message and then cut it out to form a strip. Layer it on decorative papers on top of a piece of white card stock. Cut out a long rectangular shape and punch a hole in the top. Add decorative eyelash fringe.

9 Place the stamped tag and strip tab into the smaller pocketed one to see how they look. Make any adjustments or add another tag if you wish. Punch a hole at the top of the pocketed tag, and add ribbon or eyelash fringe. Set aside momentarily.

10 Open out the card and use the needle to punch a hole on the front of the card underneath each of the diagonally cut corners, about ½ inch from the edge.

It's My Birthday (Suit!) Invitation

Sort through old photos and expose your true self through a clever birthday invitation! Your dearest friends will love it because, of course, they have similar funny photos tucked away in a drawer.

materials

Old photograph of your choice

Colored card stock (for photo backing)

Heavy book

Printer-compatible vellum

Glue stick

Tags

Eyelets

Embroidery floss, cord, or ribbon (for attaching tags)

Envelopes

tools

Computer, scanner, and printer

Scissors

Decorative-edge scissors

Awl

Eyelet-setting tool

Small hammer

process

1 Scan your photograph. Size the photo so that it's the size you want for your final card, leaving a ½-inch border around the image. Repeat it so that several copies of the photo fit on standard printer paper. Print out as many sheets of duplicate images as you need for your cards.

2 Glue the images to pieces of card stock and weigh them down while they dry so that they're flat. Use a pair of decorative scissors to cut the edges of the card, leaving a nice margin around the photo so that it resembles an old photo.

3 Print out lines of text on printer-compatible vellum to attach to the photo diagonally and to glue on the tag. (You can put a message on the photo announcing your party and put the dates and time on the tag.)

4 Use eyelets to attach the printed text to each of the cards. Trim the tag text to fit the tags, and glue each message in place.

5 Tie the tags to the invitation with embroidery floss, cord, or ribbon. Place each invitation in an envelope.

materials

Photographs of your favorite dishes

Blank postcards (4 x 6 inches)
  or greeting cards (larger than
  4 x 6 inches)

Adhesive made for photos that is
  archival and non-yellowing

Colored paper for printing recipe

tools

Heavy book

Scissors

Favorite Recipe Greeting Cards

This "recipe card" lends new meaning to that familiar phrase. Dish out your favorite concoctions, photograph them, and make a card to send to a friend. You can use a postcard or a regular folded card.

process

1 Choose a recipe to share and make the dish. Surround it with a place setting or other decorative items of your choice. Take well-lit photos and have the images processed on 4 x 6-inch paper. Matte paper works well for photographs and creates a nice looking card.

2 Choose your favorite version. Use photo-safe adhesive to glue it on a 4 x 6-inch postcard or the front of a larger blank greeting card. Press the card under a heavy book while it dries.

3 Copy the recipe on colored paper so it fits within a 3 x 5-inch space. If you're making a postcard, leave room for the address and stamp. If you're placing the recipe inside a card, you can fill the space. You can write the recipe by hand or type and print it out from a computer.

4 Trim the edges so that it fits the back of your postcard or inside your card.

5 Adhere it and allow it to dry.

Dinner Party Invites

These clever invitations collaged with bits and pieces of commercial packaging spice up any dinner gathering. If you're not doing Italian, use your imagination to come up with other combinations.

materials

Labels from canned goods, wine bottles, or pasta packages

Brown kraft paper cards and matching envelopes

Glue stick

Alphabet stamps and inkpad

Color copies of collaged image (optional)

Foil bottle-toppers from wine bottles for decorating envelopes (optional)

tools

Scissors

process

1. Choose several images and/or designs from your labels to use on your invitation.

2. If you're making a lot of cards, you can repeat the same images (if you've collected enough labels) or vary the collages from card to card. Or make one dynamite-looking collage and replicate it in the form of color copies.

3. Cut out the images. Arrange them on the blank canvas of your card and decide on placement. Be creative, thinking about what you want to "say" with these visual elements.

4. Use alphabet stamps on brown paper to print a message for your party, and cut out the message. Add this to your design in a prominent place. When you're satisfied with how things look, glue all the pieces into place.

5. Continue to duplicate your design or make varied collaged cards. Or replicate one card that you like by making color copies. If you use this method, cut out the pieces and glue them into place, leaving brown paper showing behind them to create the appearance of a collage.

6. If you wish, enclose the menu for the dinner party inside along with the other information about the party (date, time, map, and so forth).

7. Use the foil bottle-topper as a decorative element on your envelope, tying the theme together.

Vellum Overlay Party Invitation

Hints of cheerful color show through this card's vellum layer printed with a
tea party image. Don't be surprised when everyone you've invited shows up
after receiving this delightful invitation!

materials

Original drawing, clip art, or template
(see page 140)

Cards with matching envelopes

Laser-compatible paper vellum

Artists' acrylic paints

Embroidery floss

Silver beads

tools

Computer and laser printer

Scissors

Stenciling paintbrush

Paper clips

Embroidery needle

process

1. Scan an original drawing or the template into your computer. Size it to fit the front of your card. Print out as many copies as you need on the vellum. Trim the pieces to card size and set them aside.

2. On the front of the card, use a stenciling paintbrush to dab on bright polka dots of acrylic paint. You might want to create a random pattern or place color behind a particular form to emphasize it.

3. When the paint has dried completely, open the card out and place the cut vellum on top of it, matching the edges. Use paper clips to hold it in place for sewing.

4. Thread the needle with embroidery floss, and pierce through the card and vellum from the inside of the card at two points along the fold equidistant from the edges. Then push the needle through one hole on the front of the card and bring the thread up through the second hole.

5. From the front of the card, pull the threads up so that they're even, and tie them in a knot close to the fold. Thread a silver bead onto one of the threads and tie both threads off on top of the bead. Trim the threads to create nice frayed ends. Carefully fold the card in again.

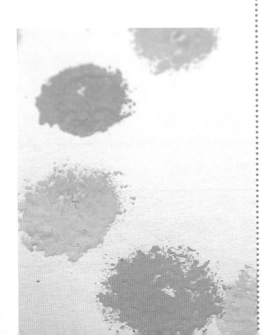

remember when...

imagine

Happy Birthday

Birthday Tag Card

A tag added to the face of a card makes a pretty birthday greeting.
Scrapbooking materials are used by the designer to give it a sophisticated look.

materials

Contrasting decorative papers

Square card and matching envelope (the one shown measures 6 x 6 inches)

White craft glue or glue stick

Scrapbooking ribbon printed with wording

Heavy card stock (for tag)

Metal scrapbooking embellishment printed with message

Small faux gems

Decorative eyelets

Square metal-rimmed vellum tag

Narrow ribbon

Glitter

tools

Scissors

Craft knife and cutting mat

Metal ruler

Awl

Small hammer

Eyelet-setting tool

Small daisy punch

Hole punch

Computer

process

1 Cut a piece of decorative paper to fit the lower half of the card, and glue it in place. Cut a contrasting piece of paper to fill the upper half of the card, and glue it in place so that the two meet in the center of the card.

2 Cut a piece of the worded ribbon that's the width of your card plus an inch. Open out the card and use your craft knife to cut a slit just slightly wider than your ribbon.

3 Thread one end of the ribbon through the slit and tack in place with glue inside the card. Glue the ribbon across the center of the card and around the edge on the other side, turning it inside the card.

4 From the heavy card stock, cut out a tag that fits the front of your card, and decorate it with layered papers. Tear the edges of some of the papers to create a nice effect.

5 Glue a word embellishment to the right-hand side of the tag. Add faux gems just above the wording.

6 On the bottom strip of your tag use the awl to punch three holes. Use the hammer and setting tool to place three decorative eyelets.

7 Cut a slit in the metal-rimmed tag so that you can slip a piece of ribbon through it and wrap the ribbon around the card to hold it in place. Tie off the ribbon at the back of the tag. Punch out a daisy from decorative paper, and affix it to the vellum tag.

8 Use the hole punch to punch out two daisies from another paper and add them to the tag. Glue a bit of glitter to the center of each flower.

9 Punch a hole in the top of your tag and thread fibers through it. Use glue to attach your tag to the left-hand side of your card.

10 Print out a computer-generated greeting in a nice font. Cut several layers of decorative papers to go beneath it. Glue this stack of over-lapping papers in place.

11 Add punched paper daisies to one corner of the envelope.

Sylvia Anne Beaumont & Jeffrey Miles Wilson
request the pleasure of your company
as they

Jump the Broom!

Saturday, June 1
at 2 o'clock in the afternoon

The wedding ceremony will be held
in the garden of the bride's parents;
Regina and Arnold Beaumont
127 Woodrow Avenue

A reception will immediately follow the service

Jumping the Broom
Wedding Invitations

The African American wedding tradition of "jumping the broom" began
during slavery as a way to symbolize marriage, which wasn't allowed among slaves.
Today, this ritual is still used to celebrate the cultural heritage of African Americans.

materials

Printer-compatible vellum

Cards and matching envelopes
that are ¼ to ½ inch larger in
dimension than your card

Patterned stamp
(purchased or hand-carved)

Inkpad or ink and brayer

Lengths of natural broom

Length of ribbon

Invisible thread

Sewing needle

tools

Computer and laser printer

Sharp scissors

Needle

process

1 On your computer, compose
your invitation in a typestyle of
your choice. Size the script to fit
the card, leaving about 1½ inches
at the top for displaying the small
broom. Print out as many multiples
of this invitation on vellum as
you need.

2 Stamp the card with the
patterned stamp. (The stamp used
here is hand-carved and emulates
African Kente cloth. The ink is a
bronze water-based variety. Using
a subtle design such as this allows
the patterning to show through
as a backdrop without interfering
with the invitation's message.)

3 With sharp scissors, cut a
bundle of broom strands about
the width of your card, leaving one
end frayed and the other cropped
neatly. Pull the ribbon up on either
side of the middle of the bundle so
that you have two equal lengths if
ribbon to wrap. Wrap it around
several times (crisscrossing it) and
end with two free ends that you
can tie into a bow at the top. Trim
the broom again as needed.

4 Thread a needle with invisible
thread and sew the small broom to
the top of the invitation, sandwiching the vellum underneath it.

Love is...the joining of two halves and a lifetime of memories

Love Keepsake Card

Express love to your soul mate through this unique card, or give it as a
wedding token to your favorite couple. You can conceal personal messages
or favorite poems in the favor bag attached to card's front.

materials

Coordinating decorative papers

White card of heavy card stock

White craft glue or glue stick

Gold eyelets

⅛-inch ribbon

Heavy cream-colored card stock

Text-weight paper for printing sayings

Decorative gold charms and heart-
  shaped brads

Dimensional foam pads or dots
  (double-sided adhesive)

Organza wedding favor bag with
  drawstring

Tacky glue

White paper box for holding card

tools

Craft knife and cutting mat

Metal ruler

Scissors

Awl

Small hammer

Eyelet-setting tool

Computer

process

1 Tear two different sheets of decorative paper diagonally and position them on the card, leaving about ¼-inch gap between them. Glue them in place, and use the craft knife to trim them to fit the edges of the card.

2 Mark the placement of the eyelets about ½ inch apart down on either side of the gap and use the awl to punch holes through the front of the card at these points.

3 Place the eyelets at ever so slightly different distances apart so that the interlaced ribbon stitching looks more handmade.

4 Use the hammer and eyelet-setting tool to set the eyelets.

5 Cut a piece of ribbon about four times the length of the measurement of your card from the right upper corner to the lower left corner. From inside the card, thread the length of ribbon through the two top holes on the right top corner.

6 Crisscross the ribbon and thread it back down through the next set of eyelets and then back up again and so forth, until you reach the other side of the card. Tie a nice little bow at the end.

7 Cut the heavy cream card stock into rectangular pieces that measure about 4 x ¾ inches each. Use a calligraphic font to print out four lovely messages on text-weight paper that will fit across each piece of card stock. If you wish, use colored ink that coordinates with your decorative papers.

8 Cut pieces of decorative paper to fit underneath the messages and glue them in place on the rectangular pieces, leaving a nice border. Then trim the messages to fit neatly on top of these papers, leaving a blank space at the end of each message so that you can attach charms and brads later on. Glue the messages on top of each cream card.

9 Attach a charm to each saying with a heart-shaped brad.

10 Cut out a rectangular piece of decorative paper for the piece shown at the top of the card. Print out a message in the same calligraphic font and color onto the text-weight paper and trim it to fit the top of the card. Layer it on top of a piece of decorative paper slightly larger to create a colored frame around the piece. Glue the two pieces together. Mount the piece at the top of the card with the foam pads.

11 Add some of the heart-shaped brads as embellishments to your favor bag.

12 Attach the bag to the card with a bit of tacky glue. Place the saying in the bag, and draw the string to hold them in place until your recipient is ready to loosen it and read them.

13 Place the dimensional card in the white box. Tie a matching ribbon around the box to present it as a gift card.

materials

Empty heart-shaped candy box

Origami or other decorative paper

Acrylic matte medium, stick of glue, or white glue

Cutouts from magazine or other printed materials to use as decorative elements

Petals from silk flowers

Sequins or beads in colors that complement other elements

tools

Scissors

Fine-tipped marker

"Bee My Honey" Box-Card

Transform a candy box into a dimensional card. Insert a sweet message inside, and your honey won't even miss the candy!

process

1 Remove the lid from the box and place it facedown on the decorative paper. Trace around the edge twice and cut out two heart-shaped pieces of paper to apply to the top and bottom. Glue on the papers and smooth them out with your fingers.

2 Following the central axis of the heart, arrange, layer, and glue cutout paper pieces, sandwiching the petals between them. Use the marker to write a message on the box.

3 As a final touch, glue on sparkling sequins or beads to catch the light.

Unforgettable Valentine

Filling a simple heart shape with repeated words scribed in contrasting
colors makes a beautiful design. Even though the instructions are written for
this particular calligraphic version, you can emulate this design with computer
graphics, stamped lettering, or simply write words with a nice pen.

materials

Tracing paper

Blank card made for watercolor
  painting and matching envelopes

2H pencil

Low-tack artist's masking tape

Gouache paints in alizarin crimson,
  magenta, and white

Paintbrush and tray for mixing paint

Scrap paper for testing paint

Kneaded eraser

tools

Scissors

T-square

Drafting table or slanted board

2 broad-edged calligraphy pens,
  nibs, and reservoirs (size 5 is
  suggested)

process

1 Cut out a heart shape from tracing paper that fits the front of your card.

2 Open out the card and place it on your drafting table or board, using the T-square to align it with the edge. Center the heart shape and use the pencil to trace it.

3 Tape the card in place on top corners. Use the T-square to lightly rule the inside of the heart shape with horizontal lines, defining the height of your letters. (The designer used a lettering style called Uncial, which has no ascenders or descenders, allowing her to leave less space between the lines so that a nice dense pattern is formed. When you choose the style of lettering for your card, think about the overall effect that it will have on your design.)

4 Squeeze out a small amount of alizarin crimson gouache into a tray, adding a few drops of water at a time, until the paint is the consistency of light cream.

5 Test the paint in the pen to make sure it's thin enough to flow yet thick enough to retain a deep red color after drying. Mix the magenta color with a dab of white in another tray and test it in the same way.

6 Begin writing the phrase I LOVE YOU, beginning in the middle of the phrase at the top of the heart, starting with OVE YOU. Using the other pen, dipped in the pink tone, begin writing LEST YOU FORGET.

7 Repeat the phrases in the appropriate colors, breaking off the lettering where the heart shape ends. Fill up the entire heart with lettering. After the calligraphy has dried, gently erase the pencil lines.

8 To address the envelope, rule the envelope and address it using the alizarin crimson color and the same lettering style. Erase the pencil lines when the envelope is dry. If you wish, use the pink to paint a small heart to the left of the name and use your pen to outline it with the darker color.

Beaded Friendship Card

Combine bright red seed and gold bugle beads to decorate this delicate card.
The placard overlapping the closure frames a lovely wire and bead dragonfly.

materials

Cream pearlescent card stock

White embossed card stock

White craft glue or glue stick

2 red paper rosebuds

⅛-inch red satin ribbon

Tacky glue

Red card stock

Gold beading wire

Red seed beads

Gold bugle beads

Clear cellophane tape

Text-weight paper

Cream-colored envelope

tools

Scissors or craft knife and
    cutting mat

Metal ruler

Bone folder

Beading needle

Dragonfly punch

Computer (optional)

process

1 From the cream pearlescent card stock, cut a piece that measures 5 x 10 inches. With the piece in a horizontal position, measure 2½ inches inside the card from each end and draw a light pencil line. Use a bone folder to score and fold along these lines. Fold these wings in so they meet in the middle of the card.

2 Cut two 1 x 5-inch strips from the white embossed card stock, and adhere them to the outer edge of each side of the folded card.

3 Wrap the stems of the red paper rosebuds around a pen to create a corkscrew effect. Tie two small bows from the red ribbon and attach one right below each rose with a dab of tacky glue. Use a dot of tacky glue to attach each rose to the patterned part of the card.

4 Cut out a 2-inch square piece from the cream pearlescent card stock. Glue it to the left-hand wing of the card, in the center. Cut out a 1½-inch square piece from the red card stock, and glue it onto the top of the cream square. Cut one final 1¼-inch square piece from the cream pearlesent card and glue it on top.

5 Cut two pieces of gold beading wire, each 5 inches long. Thread a 2¾-inch-long strand of alternating red and gold beads.

6 Use the needle to punch two holes through the card on the left wing where the two decorative papers meet, 1 inch from the bottom and top edges. Work the ends of your wire through each hole and secure them to the back of the card with cellophane tape. Repeat on the other wing.

7 Punch four dragonflies from the red card stock, and glue one in each corner of the card.

8 To make a wire and bead dragonfly, begin with a piece of wire about 8 inches long and fold it in half. Twist the folded end of the wire to form a little loop. Slide several beads of your choice over both strands of the wire (figure 1). Twist the wire underneath the beads to keep them in place. This section will be the tail of the dragonfly.

9 Next, make a small loop with the left-hand wire. Tuck the wire behind the straight wire (figure 2). Use the same piece of wire to make a small loop on the right side of about the same size (figure 3).

10 Use the right-hand wire to make a loop on the right-hand side (figure 4). Using the same piece of wire to make a loop on the left (figure 5).

11 Loop each end of the remaining wire around the joints of the loops to tighten and secure them. Add a few more beads (figure 6). Trim the excess wire and curl the antennae. Shape the wings as you wish.

12 Attach the beaded dragonfly to the center of the card with a bit of tacky glue.

13 Print out your message on text-weight paper, or write it by hand. Cut the paper to make an insert for your card. Tack it in place inside the end to cover the beading thread on the panels.

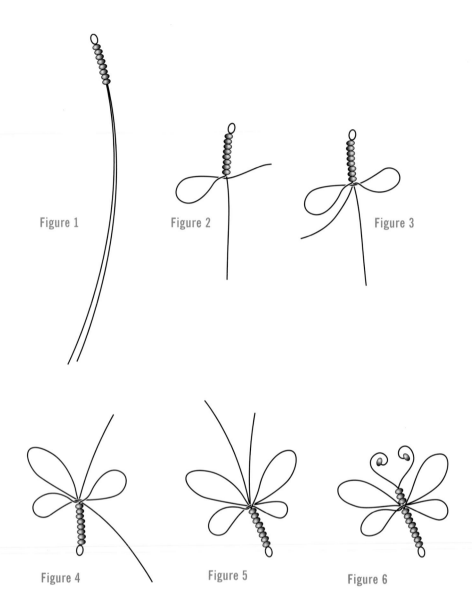

Figure 1 Figure 2 Figure 3

Figure 4 Figure 5 Figure 6

Stenciled Photograph Cards

Alter your favorite photographs by stenciling them with simple shapes and cutting them out. Adhere them to cards for a unique and unexpected look.

materials

Photographs processed with a matte finish

Stencils in shapes of your choice, such as animals or flowers

Low-tack masking tape

Decorative background papers (optional)

Adhesive made for photos that is archival and non-yellowing

Blank cards

Envelopes

Fabric paint (optional)

tools

Scissors or craft knife

Heavy book

process

1 Try out various combinations of photographs and stencils by holding them up to bright light to give you an idea of how they'll look together.

2 When you're satisfied, use masking tape to hold the stencil in place on the back of the photograph. Trace around the shape before removing the tape and stencil.

3 Cut out the shape with scissors or a craft knife.

4 Use a decorative paper as a background underneath the photo. Glue the paper in place, and allow it to dry under a heavy book before you adhere the photo.

5 Glue the stenciled photograph on your card, and smooth it out. If you wish, try using fabric paint to accent photograph.

Beeswax "Poppet" Cards

This designer calls her whimsical paper collage characters "poppets."
Here she's adapted this fun idea to a trio of cards. You can make a poppet group
or simply make one. For fun, use old family photos for the faces.

materials

Photocopies of old photographs

Watercolor paper

Black drawing pen

Decorative tissue papers

100% bleached beeswax

Wax crayons

Cardstock or scrapbook papers

Glue stick

Envelope template (page 141)

tools

Scissors

Travel iron (with no steaming holes)
or small quilting iron

process

1 Make photocopies of faces you've selected for your cards, enlarging or reducing them as needed. If you're creating a group or family, make the heads proportional with one another.

2 Cut out one of the faces. Trace it onto a piece of scrap paper, and sketch a body to go with it until you're satisfied with the shape. It need not be more than a very general shape since you'll add details later. Cut out this template and trace it onto the watercolor paper.

3 Fold the paper along the left edge of the body. Cut out the card, beginning at the edge of the fold and around the edges that are not part of the fold.

4 Use a black drawing pen to outline the body and add clothing elements such as collars, aprons, buttons, or pockets.

5 Trace the body onto decorative tissue paper and cut out the shape, which will serve as the clothing. Slip a piece of blank paper inside your card to protect it from wax seeping inside and leaving stains.

6 Position the tissue paper on the front of the card. Heat up the iron and hold a chunk of beeswax to it, allowing the wax to dribble onto the body portion of the card. Use the iron to move the beeswax around and place the decorative tissue on the surface. Dribble more wax on top of the tissue and smooth it with your iron.

7 If you wish, add more layers of decorative tissue since the beeswax won't cause the tissue colors to run.

8 If you'd like to add color to fill in a collar or other detail, use a wax crayon. As you did before, hold the crayon to the iron and allow the wax to drip before smoothing it onto areas that you want to color. For example, you can fill in an apron with white by covering a larger area and smoothing out the wax, or add small dimensional details such as buttons using wax drops.

9 If you need to correct something, heat up the crayon wax with your iron and wipe it off with a paper towel. And to create more texture on the piece, dribble more beeswax on top of your final design.

10 To create a house-shaped envelope, cut out the template and trace around it on cardstock or other decorative paper. Cut out, fold, and glue it as indicated. Decorate your house envelope with ink-drawn lines and cut-outs from other paper.

Happy Baby Card

This whimsical card welcomes a new baby with a delightfully clever look. It makes use of a baby button and accordion-folded paper.

materials

Card stock in yellow, pink, and blue

1-inch-wide pink ribbon

Baby button or scrapbook trinket

Self-stick alphabet letters

Envelope template (see page 140)

2 Eyelets

Embroidery floss

tools

Bone folder

Scissors

Craft knife and cutting mat

Tacky glue

Small hole punch (optional)

Eyelet tool

Double-sided tape

process

1 Decide on the size of your card, and cut out a piece of blue card stock, doubling the width in the direction of the fold. Fold the card in half and use a bone folder to smooth the edge.

2 Cut a piece of yellow paper that's about 1 inch less than the height of your card and the width of it plus about 2 inches (to allow for folding). Fold the paper into an accordion at about ¼-inch intervals. Place the folded paper on your card and see if it fits. Trim it if needed.

3 Use the craft knife to cut two 1-inch slits in the valleys of the folds at the top of the yellow accordion. Thread a piece of pink ribbon through the slits from the front, and overlap the ribbon on the back of the piece. Attach the ribbon ends with a dab of tacky glue.

4 Cut a piece of yellow card stock the same size as the accordion. Glue the accordion in place on top of this piece to give it stability.

5 Add loops of pink ribbon on top of the threaded ribbon to form a bow. Glue the ribbon in place in the center of the background ribbon.

6 Cut two oval pieces from the pink and blue papers, making the pink one about ⅛ inch larger in diameter. Layer the ovals and glue them together.

7 If you're using a button with a tab on the back, use the hole punch to punch a hole in the center of the ovals for holding the tab. Place the button or trinket. Adhere it to the ovals with tacky glue.

8 Cut a piece of pink paper to hold the stick-on letters conveying your message.

9 Place both the ovals and the message on the card, and adhere them to the accordion piece.

10 Glue the whole piece (baby and all) to the front of your blue card.

11 To make the envelope, enlarge the template and use it to cut out a piece of blue card stock. Fold the lines as shown. Fold the card together with the side panels on the inside, overlapping them slightly.

12 Cut two small circles of yellow paper for the closure and place them as shown in the finished photo: one on the edge of the top flap and one beneath the flap on the overlapped side panels. Hold them in place on the envelope with a tiny bit of glue and let it dry.

13 Thread an eyelet with floss and set it in the middle of the top circle on the top flap. Set the second eyelet in the middle of the bottom circle that overlaps the flaps so that this portion of the card is held together.

14 Place bits of double-sided tape on the back of the bottom flap. Press the flap in place on top of the side flaps to further reinforce the envelope. Since this envelope has a ½-inch depth, your card should slide in easily.

Congratulations on your new arrival

New Arrival Card

This distinctive card is personalized with the name of the recipient's new baby.
Don't be surprised if it gets framed and hung on the wall as a keepsake.

materials

Decorative baby-theme scrapbooking papers

Square card and matching envelope (the card pictured measures 6 x 6 inches)

White craft glue or glue stick

½-inch-wide colored ribbon

Heavy card stock in metallic color (silver or gold)

Text-weight paper

⅛-inch-wide colored ribbon

Wire rim vellum tag

Metal scrapbooking charms with baby theme

Black fine-tipped marker (optional)

Blank circular polymer clay beads or preprinted alphabet beads

28-gauge wire

Seed beads

Swatches of mulberry paper

tools

Scissors

Craft knife and cutting mat

Metal ruler

Computer

process

1 Cut two pieces of decorative paper for the front of your card, one that fits the upper half and one for the lower half. Glue them in place. and let them dry.

2 Cut a length of the ½-inch ribbon that's about 2 inches longer than the width of the card. Open out your card and use your craft knife to cut a 1-inch slit in the card's spine where the two papers overlap. Slide about an inch of the end of the ribbon through the slit, inside the card. Glue the ribbon down across the overlapped papers. Tuck the remaining ribbon inside the card, and glue it down.

3 Use your craft knife and a metal ruler to trim a 2½ x 2½-inch square from the metallic card stock. Glue it onto the middle left-hand side of your card on top of the ribbon. Then cut a slightly smaller rectangular piece from coordinating paper and layer it on the square.

4 Use a nice font to print out a greeting on a piece of text-weight paper, and trim around the lettering to form a strip. Cut a piece of metallic card stock to fit beneath it and a piece of decorative paper to layer between the two. Mount this piece on the bottom left-hand side .

5 Thread one end of a 4-inch piece of colored ribbon through one of the holes on the vellum tag. Thread on one of the metal baby charms and thread the remaining ribbon back through the other hole. Use glue to attach the tag to the right-hand side of the card.

6 Use the black pen to write the baby's name on the polymer beads and allow them to dry, or select the letters from your pre-printed alphabet beads.

7 Make a circle with your wire that fits within the square on the left. Cut the wire, leaving some extra wire to work with. Thread about an inch of seed beads onto the wire and then add a metal charm. Add letter beads with a seed bead in between each of them, finishing off with another metal charm and 1 inch of seed beads.

8 Twist together the ends of the wire to fasten it. Trim off any excess wire. Tie a couple of lengths of the thin ribbon at the top of the ring.

9 Layer a piece of mulberry paper beneath the ring on the square. Attach the two pieces with glue, and allow everything to dry thoroughly.

10 Decorate the outside of the matching envelope with a swatch of torn mulberry paper and a charm tied with a bit of ribbon. Layer and glue in place to give a hint of the contents!

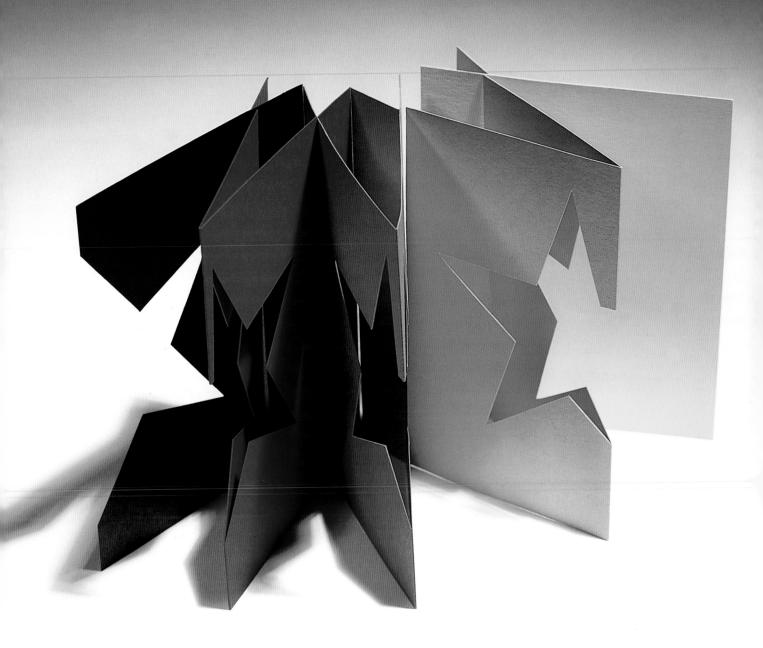

Multi-Star Pop-Up

Give this fabulous pop-up greeting as a token of congratulations or celebration.
Each star is slightly shifted in the configuration, creating a carousel-like effect.

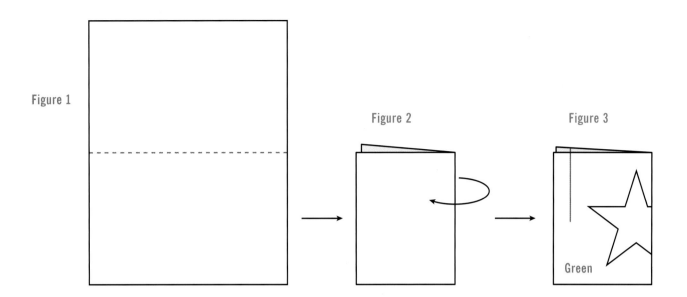

Figure 1

Figure 2

Figure 3

Green

materials

8½ x 11-inch sheets of card stock in five colors: green, red, light blue, dark blue, and yellow

Envelope that is 5 x 6 inches or larger

tools

Metal ruler

Craft knife and cutting mat

Bone folder

Photocopy machine

Clear cellophane tape

process

⚙ Fold each of the card stock pieces in half, as shown in figure 1. Cut them in half along the fold line. Fold each color in half lengthwise as shown in figure 2 and crease it with the bone folder. Leave the light blue, green, and red papers doubled. Cut along the fold line of the yellow and dark blue papers to produce a single layer of paper.

⚙ Enlarge each of the stars shown in the figures 3 through 6 to fit the colored papers. Cut them out, and trace each onto the color indicated. Carefully cut out each star from each paper to leave a negative space.

⚙ As indicated in the diagrams, cut 2¾-inch slits from the top down, 1 inch from the edge, on the green and red pieces. Cut slits of the same size from the bottom up on the light blue, dark blue, and yellow pieces. This cut is slightly past the halfway mark, making the card easier to put together later.

Figure 4

Red

Figure 5

Light Blue

Figure 6

Dark blue

Figure 7

Yellow

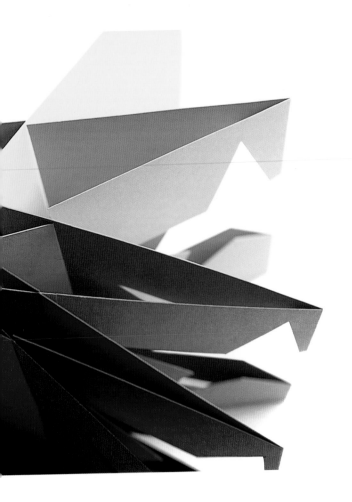

4 Tape together the colored sections on the back as indicated on the template diagrams (figure 8).

5 Once the pieces are taped, fold them to form accordion-like shapes. Position the red and green piece on the bottom with the slits positioned up and the other piece above it with the slits positioned down. Study the template diagram and slide together the slits that match by letter designation (a, b, c, and d).

6 Patience and gentleness are required to put this piece together! Go at it carefully and slowly so that you don't damage your paper pieces.

Figure 8

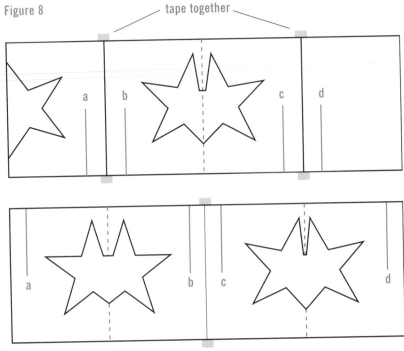

Festive Holiday Tags

Plain tags from an office supply store can be transformed into elegant gift tags with a few brightly patterned scrapbook papers, trims, and some unusual ties.

materials

Heavyweight scrapbooking papers in various decorative patterns

Paper tags (from office supply store or craft store)

Glue stick

Scrapbooking seals (optional)

Fine wire mesh and hot glue (optional)

Beads of your choice, such as seed beads and tubular beads

Beading thread

Eyelets

Ribbon or craft wire

tools

Scissors

Beading needle

Hole punch

Eyelet-setting tool

Small hammer

process

1. Cut pieces of scrapbooking paper to fit one side of each tag and glue them in place. Trim the edges so they're even.

2. Adhere a decorative piece of your choice, such as a scrapbooking seal, to the front of the tag. As another option, cut fine wire mesh and use hot glue to hold it in place on the tag.

3. Through the paper tag, stitch beads in a pattern of your choice on top of it. Tie off the ends of the thread on the back.

4. Apply decorative paper to the other side of the tag and trim the edges. If you have sewn on beads, this paper will cover up any threads.

5. Punch a hole at the top of each tag and set an eyelet in it. Thread each tag with a generous length of ribbon or craft wire.

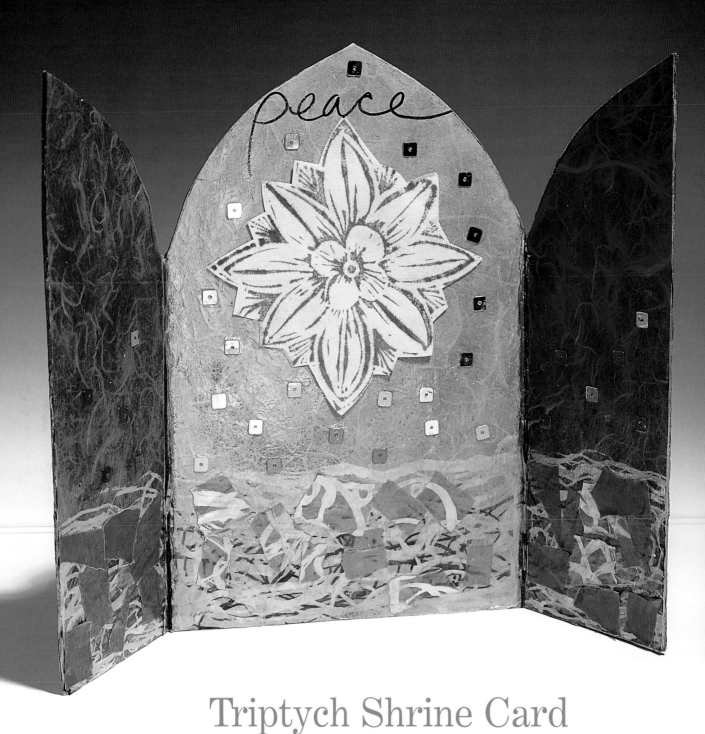

Triptych Shrine Card

This card is a piece of art that will be cherished by its recipient for many years to come. In candlelight, its textures and reflective materials come to life.

materials

Template (page 141)

Black illustration board

Red mulberry paper

Acrylic gloss medium

Rubber stamp and ink pad

Sheet of white paper for stamping

Swatches of decorative papers,
tissue paper, or magazine pages

Metallic markers, gold and silver

Acrylic paint in color of your choice

Artist's paintbrush

Black permanent marker

Sequins

tools

Craft knife

Scissors

Metal ruler

Artist's paintbrush

process

1 Cut out the template and trace it on the black illustration board. Cut out the shape with a craft knife.

2 From the red mulberry paper, cut out a piece that fits the back of the center of the shrine. Also, cut two pieces of paper that fit the wings, with a slight margin added to the inside edges so they overlap the hinges, lending them reinforcement.

3 Paint a coat of acrylic gloss medium on the back of the shrine and adhere the center paper to it. Glue down the two cut pieces of paper that fit the wings. Coat the papers with gloss medium, adding a bit of shine to them. Allow this side to dry completely.

4 Flip the shrine over and trace the outline on red mulberry paper before cutting it out. Glue the red paper down on this side of the shrine. Allow it to dry.

5 Create the top design element by stamping it on the piece of white paper and cutting out the shape. Randomly tear up bits of decorative paper and put them aside. Now you're ready to paint and collage the inside of the piece.

6 Use a dry-brush technique to scumble several layers of paint onto the inside central panel, allowing a bit of the red to show through. After the paint dries, place the central design element and glue it on. Randomly collage bits of torn paper on the bottom of the piece to create a feeling of movement. If you wish, scribble lines on top of the paper and use the metallic marker and gray paint to add more lines.

7 Add sequins around the stamped image, scattering them as you wish to create reflective points in the piece.

8 Use the black marker to script a word at the top of the shrine.

9 As a final step, place your straightedge along each fold line. Use your craft knife to score lines about halfway through the board's thickness. Bend the sides in toward the center.

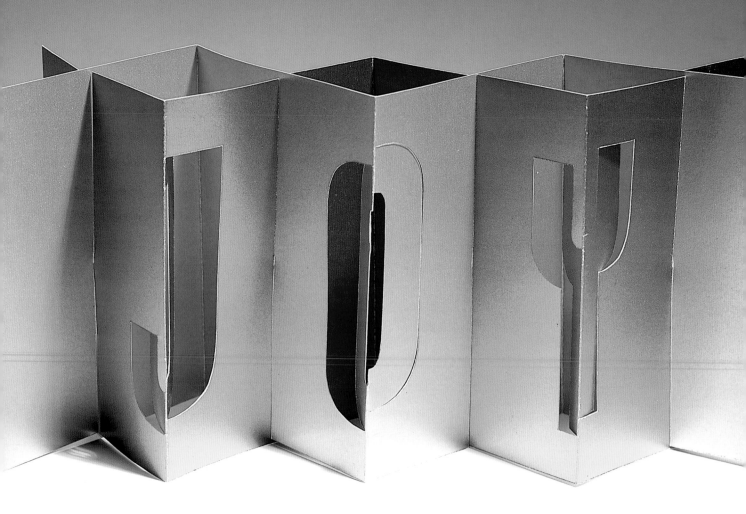

Accordion Fold JOY Card

This amazing card makes an incredible holiday gift since it doubles
as a centerpiece or decoration. If gold and silver are too traditional for you,
jazz it up by using hot pink and green!

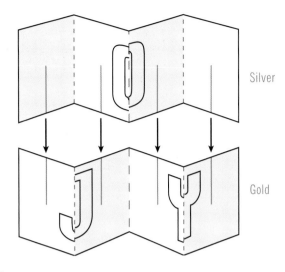

Figure 1

Silver

Gold

materials

Templates (see page 142)

Metallic gold and silver card stock (at least 17 inches long) or other colors of your choice

Tracing paper

Glue stick

tools

Long metal ruler (at least 18 inches)

Craft knife and cutting mat

Bone folder

process

1 From each of the sheets of card stock, cut a piece that measures 17 x 5½ inches.

2 Refer to the templates for the placement of the folds. Use the bone folder to score the middle fold lines on each piece on the back of the paper, and fold each in half in the direction indicated in figure 1. Score two lines halfway between the middle fold and each end of the piece on the back of the paper. Use the bone folder to fold each in the direction indicated in the figure.

3 Cut the silver panel slits where marked with the letters a, b, c, and d on the template. Pass the halfway mark slightly so that you cut each slit about 2³⁄₁₆ inches. This will make the card easier to put together later. Cut the slits on the gold panel in the same way.

4 Use the templates and tracing paper to lightly trace the lettering onto each panel. With each panel flat on the cutting mat, carefully cut out the letters. Make sure to stop at the fold. Notice that the cuts aren't lined up on purpose.

5 Fold each panel together and check to make sure that the slit lines are all cut to the same length. This will assure that the pieces fit together properly.

6 Hold the silver panel about the gold one and gently slide the two together. Once together, fold up the whole card so that the end where the word begins is on top. You'll add the dove design to this end, which will be the first thing your recipient sees. If one of the panels on this end is white and the other is gold or silver, cut out a piece of card stock in the other color to cover the white section and glue it on top.

7 Use the dove template to cut out half of the bird in one color and half in the other. Use the glue stick to adhere the shapes to the front of the card when it is closed.

8 Gently open out the card again and pull the letters out toward you before placing it on a flat surface.

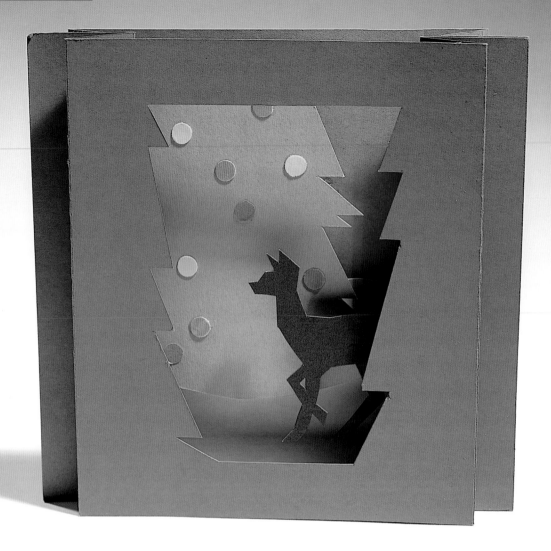

Dimensional Deer and Tree Card

This charming card might remind you of those magical pop-up books you had as a child. When it's pulled all the way out, the greeting is revealed.

materials

Card stock in dark green, light green, white, blue, dark brown, yellow, and pink

Templates (page 140)

tools

Metal ruler at least 18 inches long

Craft knife and cutting mat

Bone folder

White craft glue

Small glue brush

Toothpick

Silver metallic pen

process

1 Score, fold, and cut a piece of light blue card stock in half as shown in figure 1. Score and fold one of these halves as shown in figure 2 so that the top of the piece looks like figure 3.

2 Using the template provided, cut out the snowdrift from white card stock. Unfold the light blue piece, and glue the snowdrift onto it between the innermost folds and flush with the bottom of the card, as shown in figure 4.

Figure 2

1 in.   1 in.

¾ in.   ¾ in.

5 in.

Light blue

Figure 3

Figure 1

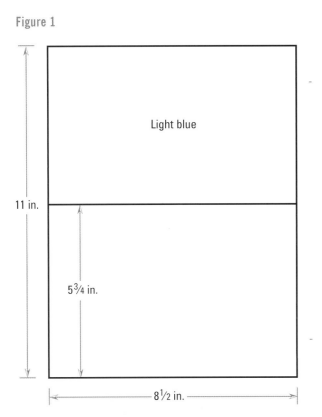

Light blue

11 in.

5¾ in.

8½ in.

Figure 4

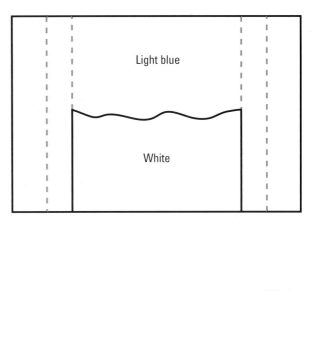

Light blue

White

Figure 5

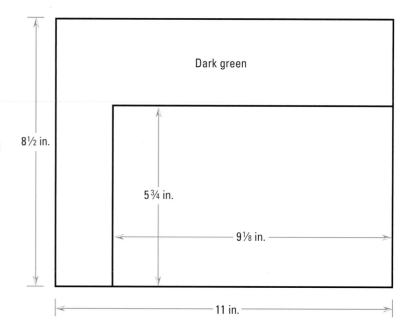

Dark green

8½ in.

5¾ in.

9⅛ in.

11 in.

3 As shown in figure 5, cut out a rectangle of dark green card stock. Score and fold it as shown in figure 6 so that the top view of it looks like figure 7.

4 Fold out the green paper so it's flat, and trace the template provided for cutting the hole on it. Cut out the hole (figure 8).

5 Trace the template provided for the Christmas tree and cut it out from light green card stock.

6 Refold the light blue piece with the snowdrift on it, and glue the tree to the left side of it, so it's flush with the top (figure 9).

7 Glue the deer onto the right 1-inch panel on the same blue piece about ¾ inch up from the bottom edge of the card, so that it shows through the cutout window.

8 Line up the folded dark green paper on top of the folded blue background piece on all four sides to make sure that the fit. Set aside the dark green panel.

9 Brush glue on one of the 1-inch panels of the blue piece only. Then glue the matching green piece to it, lining all the edges up. Proceed to the other side of the panel and repeat this, gluing the other edges together.

Figure 6

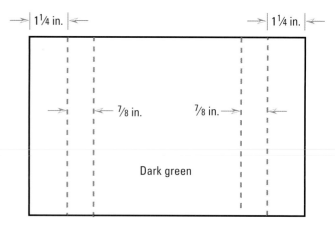

1¼ in.

1¼ in.

⅞ in.

⅞ in.

Dark green

Figure 7

Figure 8

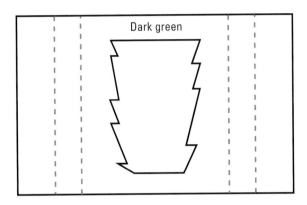

Dark green

10 Once you're done, the card should lie completely flat, and you should be able to open it by pulling the glued sides out and away from each other, revealing the inside of the card.

11 Use the metallic ink pen to scribe a simple message inside the card when pulled to its open position.

Figure 9

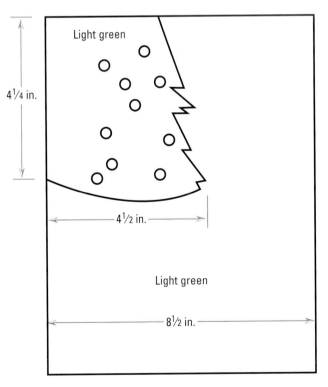

Light green

4 1/4 in.

4 1/2 in.

Light green

8 1/2 in.

Card & Envelope Templates

Enlarge to size indicated

Touch of Nature Cards, page 30

Stylish Portfolio Card, page 80

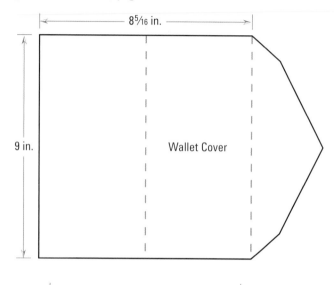

8 5/16 in.

9 in.

Wallet Cover

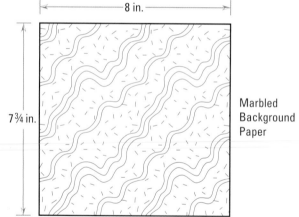

8 in.

7 3/4 in.

Marbled Background Paper

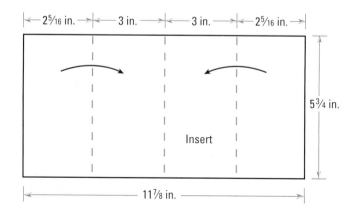

2 5/16 in. — 3 in. — 3 in. — 2 5/16 in.

5 3/4 in.

Insert

11 7/8 in.

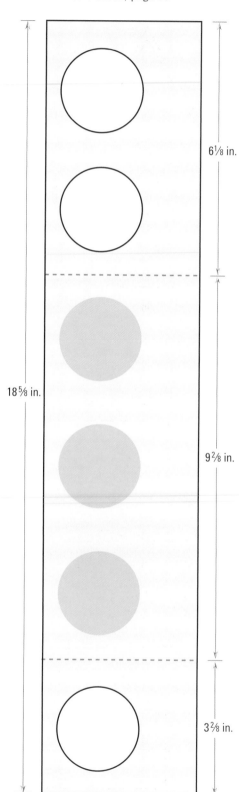

6 1/8 in.

18 5/8 in.

9 2/8 in.

3 2/8 in.

Seed Packet Cards, page 32

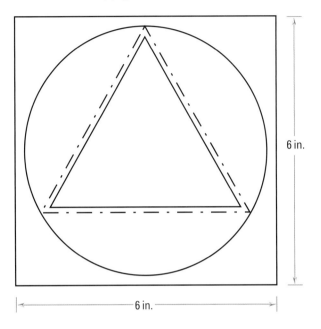

6 in.

6 in.

Black Cat Card, page 87 (actual size)

Mirrored Cards (envelope), page 82

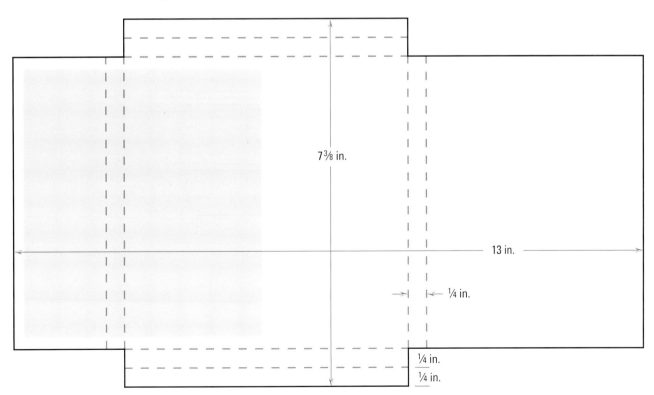

7³⁄₈ in.

13 in.

¹⁄₄ in.

¹⁄₄ in.

¹⁄₄ in.

Vellum Overlay Party Invitation, page 104
(enlarge to preferred size)

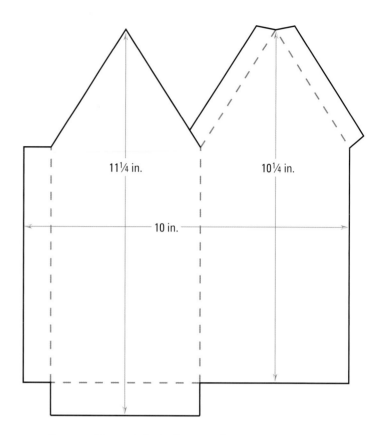

11¼ in.

10¼ in.

10 in.

Happy Baby Card, page 122

Beeswax "Poppet" Cards (envelope), page 120

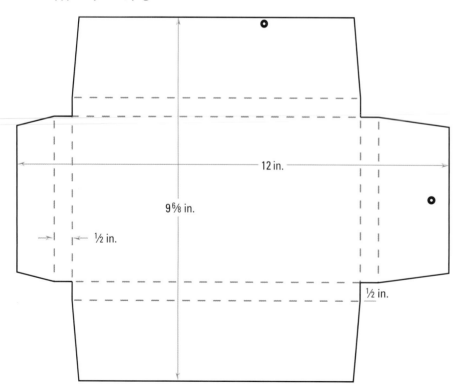

12 in.

9⅝ in.

½ in.

½ in.

Triptych Shrine Card, page 130

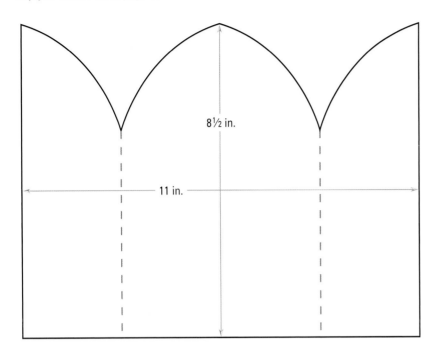

8½ in.

11 in.

Dimensional Deer and Tree Card, page 134

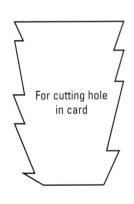

For cutting hole in card

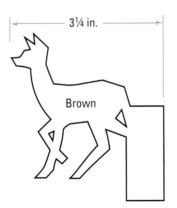

3¼ in.

Brown

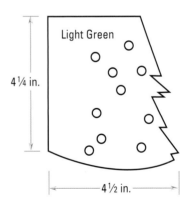

Light Green

4¼ in.

4½ in.

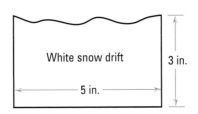

White snow drift

3 in.

5 in.

Accordian-Fold JOY Card, page 132

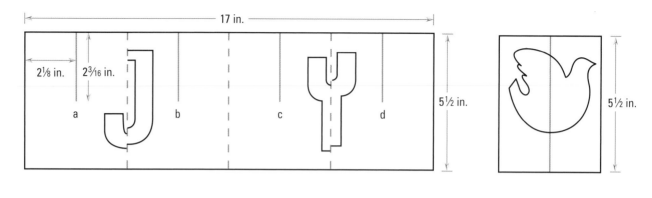

Elegant Stitched Cards (envelope), page 62

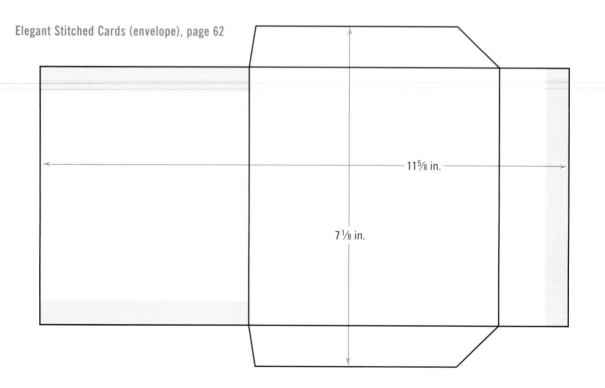

Metric Conversion Chart

INCHES	MILLIMETERS CENTIMETERS	INCHES	MILLIMETERS CENTIMETERS
1/8	3 mm	15	38.1 cm
3/16	5 mm	15 1/2	39.4 cm
1/4	6 mm	16	40.6 cm
5/16	8 mm	16 1/2	41.9 cm
3/8	9.5 mm	17	43.2 cm
7/16	1.1 cm	17 1/2	44.5 cm
1/2	1.3 cm	18 (1/2 yd.)	45.7 cm
9/16	1.4 cm	18 1/2	47 cm
5/8	1.6 cm	19	48.3 cm
11/16	1.7 cm	19 1/2	49.5 cm
3/4	1.9 cm	20	50.8 cm
13/16	2.1 cm	20 1/2	52 cm
7/8	2.2 cm	21	53.3
15/16	2.4 cm	21 1/2	54.6
1	2.5 cm	22	55 cm
1 1/2	3.8 cm	22 1/2	57.2 cm
2	5 cm	23	58.4 cm
2 1/2	6.4 cm	23 1/2	59.7 cm
3	7.6 cm	24	61 cm
3 1/2	8.9 cm	24 1/2	62.2 cm
4	10.2 cm	25	63.5 cm
4 1/2	11.4 cm	25 1/2	64.8 cm
5	12.7 cm	26	66 cm
5 1/2	14 cm	26 1/2	67.3 cm
6	15.2 cm	27	68.6 cm
6 1/2	16.5 cm	27 1/2	69.9 cm
7	17.8 cm	28	71.1 cm
7 1/2	19 cm	28 1/2	72.4 cm
8	20.3 cm	29	73.7 cm
8 1/2	21.6 cm	29 1/2	74.9 cm
9 (1/4 yd.)	22.9 cm	30	76.2 cm
9 1/2	24.1 cm	30 1/2	77.5 cm
10	25.4 cm	31	78.7 cm
10 1/2	26.7 cm	31 1/2	80 cm
11	27.9 cm	32	81.3 cm
11 1/2	29.2 cm	32 1/2	82.6 cm
12	30.5 cm	33	83.8 cm
12 1/2	31.8 cm	33 1/2	85 cm
13	33 cm	34	86.4 cm
13 1/2	34.3 cm	34 1/2	87.6 cm
14	35.6 cm	35	88.9 cm
14 1/2	36.8 cm	35 1/2	90.2 cm
		36 (1 yd.)	91.4 cm

Designer Bios

Beth Berutich *Birmingham, Alabama*
Beth is a designer and artist who has been featured in several Lark books, including *The Michaels Book of Paper Crafts*.

Jill Bliss *San Francisco, California*
Jill is an artist, designer, and founder of Blissen, a design company based in San Francisco that integrates handmade and mass-produced materials. For more information visit **www.blissen.com**.

Laura Brooks *Asheville, North Carolina*
Laura attended Ringling School of Art and The Instituto Allende in San Miguel de Allende, Mexico. Her handmade cards and books are available through specialty shops. Contact her at **laurabrooks@bellsouth.net**.

Claudine Hellmuth *Orlando, Florida*
Claudine is a nationally known collage artist, author, and workshop instructor. She is the author of *Collage Discovery Workshop* and *Collage Discovery Workshop: Beyond the Unexpected* (North Light Books). Visit her website at **www.collageartist.com**.

Maggie Jones *Statesboro, Georgia*
Maggie is a former high school art teacher. She creates artwork in her spare time, and works as a volunteer at the new Averitt Center for the Arts. Her work has been published in several Lark books.

Megan Kirby *Asheville, North Carolina*
Megan is an art director whose work has been featured in many Lark books, including *The Michaels Book of Crafts*, *The Michaels Book of Paper Crafts*, and *Altered Art*.

Claudia Lee *Liberty, Tennessee*
Claudia is a studio papermaker and instructor who is the author of *Papermaking* (Lark Books). She runs The Liberty Paper Mill, a working and teaching studio in Tennessee. Contact her at **paperlee@dtccom.net**.

Julia Lucas *Nanuet, New York*
Julia is a photographer, greeting card designer, and traditional soap maker. She won the 2002 Strathmore Photographic Greeting Card Design Contest. To see more of her work, visit **www.saturdaynightsoap.com**.

Natascha Luther *Dortmund, Germany*
Natascha works as a full-time teacher. Her stamp collection can be viewed at **www.acapella-stempel.de/11_Neuheiten_01.htm** and her artwork at **www.laraslarpkram.de/**.

Susan McBride *Asheville, North Carolina*
Susan is an art director, illustrator, and author of the children's book, *The Don't-Get-Caught Doodle Notebook* (Lark, 2005). Her work has appeared in many Lark books, including *Altered Art*, *The Artful Egg*, *Halloween for Grown-Ups*, and *Making Creative Journals*. Susan shows her personal work in Asheville, North Carolina, which is where she makes her home.

Carol Miller *Witney, Oxfordshire, England*
Carol began making cards as a hobby in 2002. After working with other crafters who inspired her to further develop her avocation, she created her own website at **www.carolmillerdesigns.co.uk**.

Akiko Sugiyama *Ormond Beach, Florida*
A native of Japan, Akiko is a nationally known collage/mixed media artist. Her work has been featured in *American Craft* magazine, *FIBERARTS*, *American Style*, and *American Artist*. She has shown in numerous exhibitions over the past 20 years.

Jen Swearington *Asheville, North Carolina*
Jen is the creator of Jennythreads silk clothing and accessories. She is formally trained in the fine arts and textiles. Her work was featured on the cover of *FIBERARTS* magazine in the September/October 2003 issue. Her work can be found at **www.jennythreads.net**.

Terry Taylor *Asheville, North Carolina*
Terry is the author of *Altered Art*, published in 2004 (Lark Books). He is also a recognized jeweler and mixed media artist.

Mary Teichman *Northampton, Massachusetts*
Mary is a printmaker, illustrator, and painter. Her etchings are found in major museum collections including The Corcoran Museum and the National Museum of Women in the Arts. Her color etchings are represented by The Old Print Shop in New York City (**www.oldprintshop.com**). View her calligraphic work at **www.mtcalligraphy.com**.

Karen Timm *Middleton, Wisconsin*
Karen is a paper, fiber, and book artist. You can see her work at **www.winnebagostudios.com**.

Nicole Tuggle *Asheville, North Carolina*
Nicole is an artist with an interest in correspondence art, collage, and assemblage. View more of her work at **www.sigilation.com**.

Luann Udell *Keene, New Hampshire*
Luann is a nationally exhibited mixed media artist and jewelry maker. She writes a column for *Crafts Business* magazine and is the author of *Rubber Stamp Carving* (Lark Books). Her website is **www.LuannUdell.com**.

Lynn Whipple *Winter Park, Florida*
Lynn is a widely recognized artist whose work has appeared in several national magazines. She is a mixed media artist who loves to work with a wide range of materials and media. Visit her at **www.whippleart.com**.

Joe Pete Williamson *Tomahawk, Kentucky*
Joe Pete studied art at the Cleveland Art Institute. She is now 93 years young and still making art. Besides painting, she enjoys the challenge of collage and making one-of-a-kind cards.

Index